Scotland
People and Places

Non-Fiction Articles

Rosemary Gemmell

Opal Scot Books

ISBN: 978-1-9162577-0-2

Scotland
People and Places

Contents

Romantic Ruins of Dryburgh Abbey — 1
A Light Across the Forth — 7
Robert Thom and the Greenock Cut — 13
Robert Burns and his Highland Mary — 19
Largs and The Vikings' Last Battle — 24
A Poor Damn'd Rascally Gager — 30
Newark Castle by the Clyde — 37
In the Footsteps of Tam o' Shanter — 42
James Watt and his Legacy to Greenock — 48
Dunfermline Abbey in Fife — 55
Dumbarton: Castle on the Rock — 60
A Day in Inveraray Jail — 67
House for an Abbot — 73
Inchmahome: Priory on the Lake — 81
Steamship Sir Walter Scott — 87
Strathspey Railway, Aviemore — 90
The Jacobite Steam Train — 94
The Lafaruk Madonna — 99
Britannia Panopticon: — 104
Britain's Oldest Surviving Music Hall

Romantic Ruins of Dryburgh Abbey

In the heart of the Scottish Borders, situated near the River Tweed, the ruins of Dryburgh Abbey nestle within a peaceful, wooded landscape safe from the turbulent wars that beset it through the fourteenth to sixteen centuries.

Although little of the abbey is now intact, the stones themselves offer a good indication of their former use and speak of the past when Dryburgh was one of the most beautiful Border abbeys. It is possible to trace its ecclesiastic history from its foundation in the mid-eleven hundreds to its demise after a sustained attack in 1544. In subsequent years, it evolved from a private home into the romantic ruins now maintained by Historic Scotland, who have provided excellent information on the abbey's past.

The first and largest of six monasteries, and home to a community of Premonstratensian canons with their white habits, Dryburgh Abbey was founded around 1150 by Hugh de Moreville, Constable of Scotland and Lord of Lauderdale, through the royal patronage of church reform. The distinctive warm sandstone used in construction would have been sourced from local quarries.

The most important building, the church, was situated on the highest ground and its ruins still provide a fine example of Gothic architecture. Entered through the once imposing west door, there is evidence that the church contained numerous windows allowing plenty of light and it consisted of north and south transepts, a nave, smaller chapels and presbytery. The crossing between was once presided over by a bell tower.

Lay people attending services in the nave entered through a doorway from the north wall. The canon's choir, at the heart of the abbey, was hidden by a *pulpitum* or screen wall and stretched to the presbytery at the east end.

The presbytery itself housed the high altar but the only evidence remaining are traces of intersecting arches supported on short pillars similar to those visible in a wall of the chapter house.

Transepts to the north and south of the central crossing provided chapel space for private devotions.

The north transept retains the most intact example of this, still standing at its full height with evidence of its elegant design and decorative carvings. Also remaining is the majestic south gable of the south transept with a window of five lancets. The surviving steps were used by the canons on the way to their night-time services. A door in the corner led down to the vestry and a spiral stair to the dormitory.

An abbey cloister provided the focal point of the canons' lives away from services. Situated on the south side to enjoy the sun's rays, it offered a place of contemplation aside from the world. A rare escape from the regimented schedule of prayers at least eight times a day, including through the night. And woe betide anyone who was late as he would be suitably punished.

Domestic life was contained within the ranges built along the east and south sides of the cloister, evidence of which is still visible at Dryburgh Abbey. One fairly intact doorway is the east processional door, one of three that linked the church and cloister. The arched, ornamental doorway clearly shows the craftmanship and grandeur of design.

Along the ground floor of the east side stood the chapter house, parlour, warming house and novices' day room, while the upper floor contained the canon's dormitory, at one time accessed by a day-stair from the cloister.

The south range, now mostly ruins, housed the kitchen and refectory, or dining room. One striking reminder of its past grandeur, however, is the impressive twelve-petal rose window in the highest point of the west gable.

A covered walkway protected the brethren from the harsher Scottish elements and provided a private study area, suggested by the shelved book-cupboard in the east wall, as well as space to walk. Although books were normally returned to the cupboard at night for safe-keeping, each year at Lent the canons were given a book from the little library which they would then spend the year reading and meditating from during *Lectio Divinia* (Divine Reading).

A sacristy, used to store items for the church services, as well as a place to don vestments, most likely stood beside the study area. Conversation in the abbey was only allowed in the parlour which was next to the sacristy. It now contains an interesting collection of carved stones.

The most important building of the abbey, apart from the church, was the Chapter House. This was the main meeting place for the canons where they received their daily news, instructions, and where they were allowed to confess any misdemeanours. As a mainly silent order, they were not allowed any casual conversation here and all business had to be conducted by addressing the whole room.

It is one of the most atmospheric and fascinating parts of the abbey, since it is largely intact, and is enhanced by the haunting medieval singing played for visitors, courtesy of a modern CD player. With a barrel-vaulted ceiling, stone benches and eleventh century arched windows, it is easy to imagine the white-robed canons sitting around the room. Some of the original painted patterns are visible at certain places. The coffins outlined on the floor mark the graves of important abbey officials, discovered in the 1700s.

Other ruins around the abbey show evidence of a warming house, where canons could sit before a fire, but it was not until the 1300s that a hooded fireplace was built. A barrel-vaulted passageway led to the novices' day room where the young men received their instructions from the master.

The once peaceful abbey life was soon disrupted through the fourteenth and fifteenth centuries, with disputes over discipline, increasing disregard for monastic orders and ultimately the continuing border wars. An information placard states that in 1322, Edward II's English army set fire to the abbey on his way back south after an unsuccessful invasion of Scotland during the Wars of Independence. There is some evidence of fire-damaged masonry at the south transept.

The ongoing disruption culminated in a raid in the 1540s when an English writer of the time records that around 1544, 700 men "rode into Scotland upon the water of Tweide to a town called Dryburgh with an abbey in the same, which was a pretty town and well buylded; and they burnte the same town and abbey, saving the churche…"

It was the end of this monastic era as neither the abbey nor town were rebuilt.

By the eighteenth century, the largely abandoned ruins of Dryburgh Abbey were given a new focus when David Erskine, 11th Earl of Buchan, bought the abbey and began to create the beautiful landscape around the ruins, planting many majestic trees. The famous Dryburgh Yew, however, dates from the twelfth century and was included in the Forestry Commission Scotland's *100 Heritage Trees of Scotland*. The earl also added some quirky touches of his own, such as an obelisk with carvings of James I and James II.

Now regarded as a romantic ruin, the abbey and grounds attracted the attention of many notable people, including Sir Walter Scott who had already gained a reputation for romanticising Scotland in his writing and whose home at Abbotsford was situated in the Borders.

Through his ancestry, Scott's final resting place was permitted within the north transept chapel he had named St Mary's Aisle, where he was buried with heart-felt ceremony in September 1832. James Morton recorded the event in *The Monastic Annals of Teviotdale* as follows:

"Never, on any occasion, was there beheld more intense feeling than when the remains of this worthy man passed through the villages and hamlets, the inhabitants of which were, in general, in mourning and standing uncovered."

One other notable person buried near to Scott's grave is Field Marshal Earl Douglas Haig of Bemersyde, who was commander-in-chief of the British Expeditionary Forces in France and Flanders during World War 1.

Wandering among these blush-pink romantic ruins in their secluded idyll beside the River Tweed, evidence of the past is everywhere and it is easy to pause a while and listen for the whispering echoes of a monastic life long gone.

Published in The Highlander Magazine (USA)

A Light Across the Forth

Stand on either side of the lower Forth estuary today and your view will immediately focus on the three magnificent bridges linking South and North Queensferry. Before these engineering giants were constructed, however, the only crossing was provided by boats.

Somewhat overshadowed by the more touristy South Queensferry, the village of North Queensferry is a fascinating Gateway to the Kingdom of Fife, and an important historical peninsula.

The name Queensferry originates from the eleventh century when Queen Margaret of Scotland established a crossing by boat at the narrowest point of the river. Although there may have been some type of ferry crossing since medieval times, it was Margaret who granted free passage to pilgrims on their way to the Holy site of St Andrews in Fife, as well as travellers to the Royal Residence at Dunfermline.

For centuries, the ferry was operated by local boatmen, who evidently proved a law unto themselves, strongly resisting any attempts at regulation on this vital link between north and south.

By 1809, the unruliness had increased. According to information provided by North Queensferry Heritage trust, action was required after reports of the "disgraceful state of disorder, irregularity and misrule". As a consequence, the government was forced to issue an Act of Parliament "for improvement of the Passage across the Firth of Forth, called the Queensferry."

Trustees were now able to establish a limited company to improve the infrastructure, in addition to operating the ferries. They subsequently engaged John Rennie, a Scottish civil engineer, who planned the new piers and buildings on both sides of the Forth. Such a busy passage required better infrastructure, with almost 300 people using the crossing in 1811.

On North Queensferry, the Town Pier and Signal House soon took shape. Now a category 'A' listed structure, the pier was originally constructed by Rennie between 1810 and 1813, thereafter being extended by the famous Thomas Telford from 1828 to 1834, to allow the larger steam-powered ships to dock.

Queen Victoria and Prince Albert made full use of it when they visited in 1842, when a red carpet was laid out to greet them. The Town Pier remained the landing stage until 1877, when the newer West Bay Railway Pier took over.

A popular ferry crossing must normally cater for passengers, as well as providing light for passing ships. Before 1817, the Signal House was the only aid for both. Passengers were allowed to wait in the downstairs room if necessary, while upstairs contained the office of Captain Scott RN, first Superintendent of the Queensferry Pass.

During the 1800s, thirty-six men and boys were employed to crew the boats on this popular crossing on the Forth. A Table of Freights on the information sheet provided by the North Queensferry Heritage Trust outlines the cost levied on each item carried across the river, according to its size and weight. One example is the 'hearse' or 'mourning coach' which was the most expensive at ten shillings.

But what of the warning light on such a busy crossing? In 1812, Robert Stevenson had been hired as a consultant by the Trustees of the Queensferry Passage to install a light as a beacon for ferry boats. This was originally situated at the top of the newly constructed Signal House, standing at the head of the Town Pier. A few years later it moved to its own small light-house where it offered even more light to passing travellers.

The Smallest Working Lighthouse

In 1817, the original light was moved from the Signal House to its present location: at the top of the new hexagonal stone tower. The fifteen-foot tower was constructed from local sandstone and its twenty-four steps are cleverly wrapped around a central smoke flu.

The octagonal light-room on top added another eight feet to its height. This new position offered better illumination of the Town Pier. During the dark nights of the 1800s, this shining beacon would have been a welcome light to the many passengers crossing the Firth of Forth.

According to the Heritage Trust information, Records of 1811 offer an indication of the numbers and types of cargo:

5769 stagecoaches and carts

44,365 horses, cows and sheep

5520 bulk barrels

83,220 foot passengers

Before 1780, the only indoor sources of light were candles or open oil lamps. Lighthouses used an open fire in a metal brazier to create their warning beacon. Oil lamps, however, needed constant attention. They used nothing but a shallow dish with a sloping wick held in a spout. Not only dangerous, they were smoky, burned poorly and offered minimum light.

Improvement arrived in 1780, when Swiss scientist, Ami Argand, patented a series of alterations to the oil lamp. His design provided a reservoir which maintained a constant feed of oil, while a cylindrical wick allowed air to flow through and around the flame. As well as increasing the intensity of light, it also reduced the smokiness. A glass chimney enhanced the air flow even more. The design was so successful it was adapted for lighthouses.

It was often regarded as a difficult, lonely job, although the lighthouse keepers at North Queensferry had it a little easier than most, especially since they did not have to live in the lighthouse, which was on dry land and easily accessed. In 1823, Robert Stevenson had published a list of instructions for the Bell Rock Lighthouse keepers, stretching to thirty-five paragraphs!

At North Queensferry, duties usually included the following:

Maintaining an adequate stock of oil in the storage tank.

Filling the lamp oil reservoir daily.

Cleaning the windows, glass chimney, and the silvered reflector.

Checking the lamp wick, trimming or replacing it as necessary.

Lighting the lamp and adjusting the wick to bring the flame to 'standard flame height', which could take up to twenty minutes if the oil was poor quality.

The light would now burn all night, guiding all who crossed the Queensferry Passage.

This smallest working lighthouse in the world, situated at North Queensferry, managed to contain a few comforts for the keeper within its clever design. On the ground floor, the oil storing tub was built into the staircase while a small stove provided warmth. It is now operated with rape seed vegetable oil, replacing the whale oil of the past!

Although the iconic Forth Rail Bridge was built in 1898, the ferry still crossed the Forth until the construction of the Road Bridge in 1964. Today's travellers can still climb the short height of twenty-four winding steps to the light-house at certain times of the year. They might even be lucky enough to light and adjust the flame of the wonderful replica lamp, and receive a Certificate of Competence for the pleasure of stepping into the past.

Published in The Highlander Magazine (USA)

Robert Thom and the Greenock Cut

Situated in the hills above the Scottish west coast town of Greenock, the historic aqueduct known as the Greenock Cut is testament to the creative innovation of 19th century civil engineer, Robert Thom.

Born in Tarbolton, Ayrshire in 1774, Thom worked as a 'wright' (joiner) in Glasgow while studying maths and engineering at evening classes.

From the age of twenty, however, he took an interest in cotton spinning and subsequently became a director of Rothesay Cotton Works on the Isle of Bute. It was on the island that he developed his innovative use of aqueducts to supply clean water for drinking and industry.

Aware of the desperate need for a clean drinking water supply to the people of Greenock, as well as its tremendous potential to the growing industry, Thom turned his attention to the rain-soaked moorland and hilly area above the town. He had recognised that the abundant rainfall combined with the natural gravity from the hills, could provide a limitless supply of clean, natural energy that would benefit all.

In 1825, the Shaws Water Company was formed by an act of Parliament to supply Greenock with water and Thom began work on the Greenock Cut that same year. On 15th April 1827, the construction of the Great Reservoir, the Compensation Reservoir and the Cut (main aqueduct) was finally completed.

The excavation involved building twenty-three small bridges over the canal-like structure while two bothies at the side provided basic accommodation for the men who kept the aqueduct free of snow and ice. Ahead of his time in harvesting such natural energy in an area of wild moorland, Thom's aqueduct finally stretched for about 5½ miles, carrying water from the Great Reservoir, named Loch Thom in his honour, all the way to town.

A series of 'falls' served eleven mills and factories, each with its own water wheel. The water dropped from one wheel to the next in a clever recycling of energy and working hours were timed to coincide with when the water power was available. Ten times cheaper than steam power, the falls on the eastern side of the cut were evidently unique in Scotland.

Thom's design involved a system of self-regulating 'wasters' to make sure the water level and supply remained constant. Fully automatic, the safety valves used a system of weights, buckets and pulleys to release excess water from the Cut during heavy rainfall. If the water exceeded a predetermined level, it activated the mechanism in the waster and the sluice opened to release the excess, thus avoiding damage to the banking. The sluice closed once the water reached a safe level again. Two of the old automatic wasters could still work as well today, proving the quality of Thom's design.

In the early nineteenth century, diseases such as typhus, cholera and smallpox were a major problem due to lack of proper sanitary conditions in the highly populated towns, killing hundreds of people of all ages.

Robert Thom was careful to ensure the purity of the water that would reach the people of this west coast town for the first time in its history. He designed an innovative self-cleaning system, using three slow sand filters above Greenock, each of them 50 feet long, 12 feet wide and 8 feet deep. When these clogged up, the water direction could be reversed and any build-up of sediment was washed away.

The local newspaper of the time, the *Greenock Advertiser*, carried the following article in 1827 and its rather flowery exuberance highlights the innovative importance of Robert Thom's construction:

"The 16th of April 1827, will long remain a memorable day in the annals of Greenock… To form an immense artificial lake, in the bosom of the neighbouring alpine regions, and lead its liquid treasure along the mountain summits, at an elevation of more than 500 feet above the level of the sea, till in the immediate vicinity of the town, it should be made to pour down a resistless torrent, in successive falls, for the impelling of machinery to vast extent – this, in a few words, was the magnificent conception of Mr Thom; and never, probably, did the first trial of so novel and extensive an undertaking demonstrate its capability and entire adaptation to its purpose, or excite such unalloyed and universal gratification…"

After relying on only nine wells for their drinking water, with no proper sewers, the nineteenth century inhabitants of Greenock now had clean drinking water and the thousands of machines in the great local industries of wool, flour, paper and various foundries were served by the huge water wheels that powered the flowing water from the Cut. But the population continued to grow, bringing yet more disease and deaths.

In 1845, another aqueduct, the Kelly Cut, was constructed by a further act of Parliament, plus an additional two reservoirs, to supplement the supply to the Greenock Cut by carrying additional water to Loch Thom. The Kelly Cut was so called because James III had granted the lands of Kelly to the Bannatyne farm in the 15th century, which they held for almost three hundred years. They had built the original Kelly Castle next to the Kelly Burn, but it was destroyed by fire in 1740 and never rebuilt.

The whole area of the Greenock Cut is still one of natural beauty. A nature trail of about a mile and a half takes visitors on a circular walk along past sheep grazing on heather-clad hills and moorland, offering views across the River Clyde to the Argyll mountains in Dunoon and the Isles of Bute and Arran, then down through the glen.

The Shielhill Glen itself is a Site of Special Scientific Interest due to the variety of deciduous trees such as silver birch, rowan, ash and oak. The open moorland is another SSSI, being a natural habitat of the Hen Harrier and an area important for its huge reserves of peat, a natural carbon store that helps to combat climate change.

At the start of the lower part of the trail, a plaque is attached to the entrance gate highlighting the Heritage Path for the Greenock Cut and a similar one highlights the Kelly Cut at the beginning of the upper path. In addition to the flora and fauna along the path, visitors can view the still-flowing waterfall bringing water from the reservoir loch, and the old wooden sluice at the beginning of the trail.

The Greenock Cut was in full use until 1971 when it was superseded by a tunnel and a new pipeline supplying the water from reservoir to town. The historical importance of the Cut was recognised and duly designated an Ancient Monument to ensure its protection.

A one-million-pound Heritage Lottery funded the restoration and better access project which was completed in 2007. The Visitor Centre enhances the nature trail with its informative exhibition, outlining and illustrating the original work in the nineteenth century.

A commemorative cairn was finally erected in memory of Robert Thom's outstanding design which boasts a plaque from the Institution of Civil Engineers in 2012:

Robert Thom
1774-1847

Civil and Hydraulic Engineer
designer of an innovative 'green' scheme
to supply Greenock with water fed
from Loch Thom via the 5½ mile 'Cut'
including a device which allowed the water level in
'The Cut' to be self-regulated

Greenock was fast becoming one of the largest industrial towns on the west coast in the nineteenth century, but poverty and inadequate housing was still a major problem for poorer people in Victorian Scotland.

Thanks to the vision of Robert Thom and his expertise as a civil engineer, the town's expanding population now had clean drinking water and the natural production of energy to power the great machines of industry.

Published in The Highlander Magazine (USA)

Robert Burns and his Highland Mary

"She has my heart, she had my hand,
By secret troth and honour's band!
Till the mortal stroke shall lay me low,
I'm thine, my Highland Lassie O'."

There is plenty of evidence that she existed, not least in Burns's own poetry, but there has long been speculation as to who exactly Highland Mary might be and how serious was their relationship.

I first became aware of Highland Mary as a child, when going on Sunday walks to Greenock cemetery with my mother, who was also called Mary. As we walked past the creepy old part of the cemetery, with its ancient trees, moss-covered tombstones and dark, winding narrow paths, my mother would always stop at one particular grave.

"That's where Highland Mary is buried," my mother said on every visit.

It was only as I grew older that I understood the name was entwined with that of Scotland's famous poet, and libertine, Robert Burns, and thus began an added fascination with Highland Mary.

According to research, 'Highland' Mary was in fact Mary, or Margaret, Campbell, born to Archibald and Agnes Campbell at Auchnamore Farm near Dunoon in 1763, and it was Mary's Gaelic highland lilt that evidently earned her the nickname 'Highland Mary'. Mary also lived in Campbeltown and, finally, Greenock on the other side of the River Clyde.

In her early teens Mary went as a nursemaid to Burns's friend, Gavin Hamilton, at his house in Mauchline where she met Burns, before moving to Coilsfield (Burns' Castle O'Montgomery in the song *Highland Mary*) to be a dairymaid.

Amongst the sketchy facts about her life, it was said that she was tall and fair-haired with blue eyes and it was after Burns was 'deserted' by Jean Armour that he turned seriously to Mary.

The song, *The Highland Lassie, O'* was written by Burns in the spring of 1786 and Burns himself wrote:

"This was a composition of mine in very early life, before I was known at all in the world. My Highland lassie was a warm-hearted, charming young creature as ever blessed a man with generous love." According to the same note by Burns, they met by appointment on the second Sunday of May by the

Banks of Ayr to take their farewell "before she should embark for the West Highlands to arrange matters among her friends for our projected change of life."

This 'change of life', however, was not to come to fruition. It is believed that Burns and his Mary had arranged to go to Jamaica and Mary was to cross the sea to meet Burns at Greenock to sail with him on the steamer, *Nancy*.

However, according to Burns, Mary "had scarce landed when she was seized with a malignant fever which hurried my dear girl to the grave in a few days, before I could even hear of her illness."

The suggestion that Burns had intended to take her to Jamaica seems to be given credence by the words of another song which begins, "Will ye go to the Indies my Mary, and leave auld Scotia's shore?"

There was some speculation as to the cause of death; some said it was of fever after nursing her brother, Robert who died of typhus, others said it was from premature childbirth with Burns's child.

Whatever the cause, Mary Campbell was buried in the Old West Highland Churchyard at Greenock, in 1786, in a lair owned by her relation Peter MacPherson. The mystery cause of her death was a step nearer to being solved when, in 1920, the churchyard was being destroyed to make way for industrial expansion.

Mary Campbell's grave was opened up so that her bones might be moved to a new resting place. There among the remains they found the bottom board of an infant's coffin suggesting that Mary had indeed given birth to a still-born child.

Given Burns's reputation and his obvious feelings for his highland lassie, there would be few surprises at the find. However, there is the alternative, and less romantic, possibility that some other relative's child had shared the same grave, as was often the custom.

The relationship between Burns and Mary, however, is further confirmed by the suggestion that, on that last Sunday in May where they met to plan their future, they exchanged Bibles and possibly some kind of matrimony vows.

According to ancient Scottish custom this could be effected by standing on opposite banks of a burn clasping one hand each in the running water while the other hands held a Bible. The Bible Mary gave to Burns has never been seen, however the Bible Burns gave to Mary can be seen in the Museum at Alloway. The title page of the little two-volume book bears the date 1782 and the price of five shillings and sixpence and is preserved together with a lock of Mary's hair.

Amongst all the speculation about Mary and her relationship to Burns, there have been some dissenting voices.

John Richmond surmised that Mary's morals were in fact very loose and that she was a kept woman, even going so far as to suggest that some of Burns's friends warned him against being too devoted to her, without any effect. It seems ironic that it should be Mary's character rather than the libertine Burns's which has been called into question

The Greenock Burns Club is known as The Mother Club since it claims to be the oldest Burns club in Scotland. It seems fitting that the area around Highland Mary's grave now contains plaques to her memory.

It also features a pleasant memorial garden surrounded by a low railing where romantics can gaze upon the adoring couple depicted on the stone and remember Burns's own lament for his lost highland love:

> *'And mouldering now in silent dust*
> *That heart that lo'ed me dearly!*
> *But still within my bosom's core*
> *Shall live my Highland Mary.'*

Published in The Highlander Magazine (USA) and the inspiration behind my dual timeline novel, The Highland Lass.

Largs and The Vikings' Last Battle

A pretty seaside town in North Ayrshire on the west coast of Scotland, Largs is used to hordes of day trippers arriving from large cities like Glasgow in summertime.

In the thirteenth century, however, the marauding Vikings mounted one of their largest invasion forces for what would be their final skirmish in the British Isles. And the Battle of Largs is still commemorated today.

At the height of their power, the Vikings travelled far and wide, invading the British Isles from Norway, Denmark and Sweden searching for new land to plunder.

It was only a matter of time before the Norsemen cast their eyes on Scotland, which was closer to Bergen by sea than their own Norwegian capital of

Oslo.

And so began years of raids and plunder, as well as a long-lasting connection with Scotland that left a legacy of Norse culture and place names long after the battles for supremacy ended. Orkney and Shetland were within such easy reach that they were soon overrun, and the Norse heritage is particularly evident in many of the place names and artefacts found around these islands.

The first invasion is thought to have taken place on the island of Iona in the 9th century, heralding several centuries of violent warfare that made no allowance for holy sites.

By 825, only a few monks remained on Iona after previous raids and although they knew they had little chance of survival when the longships arrived once more, they refused to move from the spiritual centre that Saint Columba had founded.

The Vikings were convinced that monasteries held hordes of silver accumulated from wealthy patrons, which the invaders intended to remove. They had no respect for holy men; instead of a cross around their neck, they wore pendants shaped as Thor's hammer, the Norse god of thunder.

There was another valuable commodity in small monastic communities like the island of Inchmarnock. The monks were well educated, often providing a centre for learning, and the Vikings discovered that human slavery was one of their most lucrative trades. Inchmarnock contained an abundance of slate and one has been found that depicts a scraped drawing of a man being dragged away by Viking warriors.

On the Firth of Clyde, the ninth century centre of the Kingdom of Strathclyde was the imposing

Dumbarton Rock which seemed impenetrable. In 870, however, the Vikings arrived and held the Rock and castle under siege for four months, until the water supply ran out and the people were forced to surrender. In addition to two hundred ships, they took many captives to be sold as slaves at auctions in Dublin and beyond.

The Norsemen themselves must have been a terrifying sight. Huge armies of helmeted warriors arriving on their unique ships, the fierce carved dragon prow raised in readiness for the raid. A new invention, these longships were designed to lie low on the water, making them fast, light and flexible to sail across the North Sea. No one was safe from the warriors: men, women, children or holy men.

It took the Norsemen two days to reach the Northern Isles of Shetland and only a little further to Orkney; by the middle of the ninth century, the islands were overrun. Orkney became the centre of the Norse World in Scotland and many eventually put down roots there, farming and introducing their own cultural heritage, some of which endures today.

By the 13th century, however, further problems arose when Scotland and Norway both came under the rule of their own kings, each determined to expand which also meant controlling Scotland.

Although Bute and Cumbrae were already under Norse rule, vicious battles ensued to rule the mainland and islands on the Firth of Clyde. A fight that would eventually end at the Battle of Largs.

The Scottish king, Alexander II, sailed up the west coast in 1249 but subsequently died, allowing the Norwegian kingdom to expand. The new king, Alexander III, then set about a brutal retaking of Scottish land, and so the skirmishes continued with neither side admitting defeat.

Outraged, the King of Norway, Haakon Haakonarson, set out with his large fleet in 1263, hoping to finally crush the Scots in the Hebrides, where local forces joined his fleet. A solar eclipse then suggested a powerful omen, but for whom?

Haakon finally led his fleet down from the Hebrides with one hundred and twenty ships and 20,000 men, achieving further allegiance as he went. The Scottish King, however, was a patient and wily man and he stalled in Ayr, waiting for the autumn weather to arrive.

Haakon demanded that the Scots withdraw as he moved nearer to the shore at Largs and the disputed areas of the Firth of Clyde. But still Alexander waited, spinning out the negotiations as he knew he couldn't defeat the Norsemen at sea.

Then on October 10th, the weather finally broke, bringing a powerful violent storm. The Norwegian fleet scattered, some driven ashore. The next morning, Haakon went ashore with 1000 men to salvage the remaining ships and cargo.

The Scots pounced at last. The Norwegian king reached safety but some of the Norsemen collapsed on the shore, with many of the longships lost, although the Norsemen finally regrouped to challenge the Scots. In the ensuing stand-off during the Battle of Largs in 1263, neither side won in the end, and the warfare was over in days.

When the weather improved and he had retrieved his stranded men, the Norwegian king burned the damaged boats. Winter was looming, supplies were few and his men were restless so they agreed to disperse and return home to overwinter in the Norse stronghold in Orkney. It is believed the king intended to wreak revenge after winter but he was old, sick and tired and finally died in the December of 1263.

Haakon was the last Norwegian king to invade Scotland and he made his peace at the shrine of St Magnus in Kirkwall Cathedral. His son had no interest in continuing the raids after five centuries of invasion and, in 1266, he renounced any claim to Scotland, for a price of 4000 marks!

Soon, the Norse descendants looked to the Scottish king for royal protection, heralding the new Scots nation.

These days, the only Norse invasion that Largs experiences is during the annual festival every August when the replica thirteenth century Viking Village is set up alongside the promenade. It provides great insight into the Viking way of life and allows modern visitors to view everything from dwelling places and cooking methods to swords and helmets, fabrics and archery.

One table could have materialised straight from

Viking times, where a young boy helped his father the Miller to grind oats on an authentic stone mill. Another longhouse welcomed visitors to touch and try on helmets and have a go at playing the ancient harp and drum. A lady was weaving wool on round wooden spindles, while another demonstrated the kind of clothes females wore.

The week-long festival culminates in fireworks and the burning of a longboat at the stone monument known as the Pencil, built in 1912, at the far end of the town near the Marina.

There is also the year-round indoor Vikingar! where visitors may experience for themselves the fascinating Viking history and culture.

For such an unassuming small coastal town, Largs has earned its place in the Viking history of Scotland.

Published in The Highlander Magazine (USA)

A Poor Damn'd Rascally Gager

"Searching auld wives barrels,
Ochon, the day!
That clarty barm should stain my laurels
But – what'll ye say!
These movin things ca'd wives and weans
Wad move the very heart o' stanes."

Robert Burns is world famous as a farmer and poet of the people, yet a large part of his adventurous life was spent as a very respectable government Exciseman, or 'poor damn'd rascally gager', as Burns himself called them. The above Extemporaneous Effusion was written on his appointment to his Excise commission in 1788 and gives an indication of Burns' mixed feelings about the post.

When the crops failed on his farm, Ellisland, in Dumfriesshire before his 29th birthday, Burns became disillusioned with farming and looked for another source of income.

Having little experience of other types of work, apart from a short time as a Flax Dresser, he contacted some influential friends in the hope of gaining their patronage in his change of career. One such man was the Earl of Glencairn, to whom Burns wrote a hopeful, pleading letter in the January of 1788, outlining his desire to be an Exciseman.

"I wish to get into the Excise: I am told your lordship's interest will easily procure me the grant from the commissioners; and your lordship's patronage and goodness, which have already rescued me from obscurity, wretchedness, and exile, embolden me to ask that interest."

It was an unpopular trade and the excisemen themselves were little liked when their job was to make sure people paid their taxes, especially with regard to alcohol. Employed by the government, it was the equivalent of today's HM Customs and Excise.

Once he had applied for a position, Burns then appealed to Robert Graham of Fintray for further patronage. They had lately been introduced at Athole House and Burns naturally took advantage of this when he had need of all the help he could get in order to attain a regular pay and security for his family:

"Sir, do I now solicit your patronage. You know, I dare say, of an application I lately made to your Board to be admitted an officer of the Excise...if I succeed, I am afraid I shall but too much need a patronising friend."

Burns was subsequently added to the roll of

excisemen in September 1789. It was a hard and often dangerous job. Covering ten parishes in his first area, Burns rode extensively, writing that he was "condemned to gallop at least 200 miles every week" and later complained: "My fingers are so worn to the bone in holding the noses of his Majesty's liege subjects to the grindstone of excise that I am totally unfit for wielding a pen in any generous subject."

The danger was real in a period when smuggling was rife, with huge profits on items such as beer, cider, brandy, tea and coffee, and Excisemen were sometimes beaten or killed. They made surprise visits to traders to check books for accurate accounts and to make sure the correct tax was applied on whisky. It certainly was not one of the most popular jobs.

As well as the roaring trade in smuggled goods there were also the elicit stills for making whisky. In the 1780s over 6000 of these stills were seized and destroyed by excisemen.

For his trouble, Burns was paid £50 per year and if he should be fortunate, or foolish, enough to catch and arrest any smugglers he earned an extra £50 and half of the captured goods. In 1790, Burns was transferred to the Dumfries Collection where he was mainly responsible for the Excise duty on goods coming into the port, such as tobacco.

There is a recorded 'moment of glory' for Burns with his intervention in the seizure of the *Rosamond*, on the Solway, when Burns evidently kept watch on the stranded smugglers while awaiting help to board the ship.

However, there are conflicting stories as to the exact proceedings with some versions talking of the ship being scuttled by her crew to avoid the goods being seized.

Whatever the correct version of events, it seems that Robert Burns was indeed involved in her capture.

According to Maurice Lindsay in his *Burns Encyclopedia*, in 1790 Mrs Dunlop, who had become a motherly friend to Robert Burns, asked Burns if her acquaintance a Mr Corbet in the Excise could be of any use in helping him get on.

Since Burns was eager to progress to the larger ports of Greenock or Port Glasgow he replied: "Were he to interest himself properly for me, he could easily, by Martinmas 1791, transport me to Port Glasgow, port Division, which would be the ultimatum of my present Excise hopes."

Burns further explained to Mrs Dunlop in 1792 that, "A Port Division is £20 a year more than any other Division, besides as much rum and brandy as will easily supply an ordinary family."

However, it was only in the Dumfries Port Division that Burns received his promotion. He moved to a town district of Dumfries in 1792, where he was able to work from his home at Mill Street, controlling brewers, tanners, chandlers and over fifty tea and wine dealers.

There is no definite evidence that Robert Burns visited Greenock, although he may have visited his Highland Mary's grave in the cemetery there during his Highland Tour of 1787, but he does seem to have visited Port Glasgow and then nearby Finlaystone Estate where his patron, the Earl of Glencairn resided.

Greenock was one of the leading sea ports in Britain in the eighteenth and nineteenth centuries, having a vast trade with the West Indies, America and Canada and was the principal customs port of the Clyde. The Georgian style Greenock Custom House was opened in 1819 and, until recently housed the Vat

Office and Gaming Taxes, as well as housing a very interesting display of Customs and Excise through the ages, including many of the items Burns would have come across in his excise work.

In pride of place on the ground floor two kilted figures sat beside an illicit whisky still, just as they would have been when Burns was searching the countryside. To complete the illusion, their story was relayed through a voice system.

The actual grey still that used to be on display originally belonged to Major General Charles Gordon, hero of Khartoum, and was made for the distillation of water in the desert. When it eventually ended up being used for the illicit distillation of spirits, it was soon seized by Custom and Excise!

The Gager himself was the original name for an exciseman and it was a skilled job, needing precision and experience. The officers had to ascertain, or gauge, the content of each cask and the quantity of liquid it contained using a variety of measuring rods, tapes, callipers and slide rules.

The resulting calculated spirit duty was then applied. The picturesque jargon used for the losses on each cask included 'slack hoops', 'leak at chimb', 'cracked stave' and 'leak at head'.

Fortunately, large containers eventually replaced the casks and, with no need for gauging, few if any officials are experienced in the skill today.

The information at the Greenock Custom House mentioned the following heart-felt verse from a gager about his cask. (The last line is Gaelic for a dram):

"Their hoops are slack
Their staves are cracked
Their heads are soft and porous

*They're leaking pints
At all their joints
Let's have a Deoch and Dorus.*"

While Burns carried out the day job, he also continued writing his poems and the fact that he was an Exciseman himself did not prevent him writing the song, *The Deil's awa wi' the Exciseman*' to the tune known as 'The Hampdresser'.

This illustrates Burns' empathy with the people in their wish to be rid of these annoying government men so they could continue drinking their purloined goods and dancing their reels. The song itself mentions various popular dances:

*"There's threesome reels, there's foursome reels,
There's hornpipes and strathspeys, man,
But the ae best dance that cam' tae the land,
Was the de'ils awa' wi' the Exciseman.*"

In his *Life of Burns*, published in 1828, Lockhart states that he had on the authority of one of Burn's fellow Excise officers that the song was written while Burns tramped the wet sands of the Solway as he kept watch on the *Rosamond* crew.

Although he never achieved promotion to the Port Glasgow division, Robert Burns seemingly was a good officer and his name was on the 'list' for promotion to supervisor, which can be seen at Greenock Custom House. There is also evidence that he acted as a temporary supervisor in Dumfries from December 1794 to April 1795.

Burns remained at his Excise station working from Mill Street until his death on 21st July 1796, still a serving officer of the Excise.

Given Robert Burns' lifestyle and reputation, it is to be hoped that the chorus of his 'Exciseman' song did not come back to haunt him:

"The de'ils awa', the de'ils awa',
The de'ils awa' wi' the exciseman,
He's danced awa', he's danced awa',
He's danced awa' wi' the exciseman."

Published in The Highlander Magazine (USA)

Newark Castle by the Clyde

Visitors travelling to Inverclyde down the M8 from Glasgow can now enjoy the impressive sight of Port Glasgow's own castle standing beside the River Clyde. It is not a new castle; it merely had lain largely hidden for many years surrounded by the shipbuilding yards that were once Inverclyde's main economy.

With the decline in local shipbuilding, the land around the castle was developed to the east in the 1980s, as Newark Park, providing a peaceful, scenic walking area with car parking, slipway and pier. This allows the castle to take pride of place once more, with the sole surviving shipyard flanking it on one side.

A well-preserved ancient monument, Newark Castle combines 15th and 16th century building. The land on which it is built first came into the Maxwell family in 1402, through marriage. However, it was not until the latter half of the 15th century that a descendent, George Maxwell, built the first parts of the castle seen today.

This originally consisted of a rectangular tower which housed the main accommodation for the family. King James IV is reputed to have stayed here in 1495, on his way to the Western Isles. At around the same period, a large gatehouse was erected, linked to the tower by a wall.

In the late 16th century, Sir Patrick Maxwell upgraded the castle and added a turreted mansion to the existing buildings, uniting the tower and gatehouse. Above the main door into the mansion, Sir Patrick's monogram is cut into the stonework. Inscribed underneath are the words, *"the blissings of God be herin"* and the date 1597.

Inside the castle there are numerous rooms to explore, connected by extremely narrow winding stairs, although a few parts are closed to the public. On the first floor, a large bright hall with windows on each side contains a magnificent Renaissance style fireplace. This was the main room of the mansion and served as the family dining room.

Immediately above, was the long gallery where people could promenade and where pictures would hang on either side. Today, part of it has been hung with interesting pictures of Newark Castle in its early years, together with scenes of old Port Glasgow. This room also contains a bust of John Wood, famous for building the steamship, the Comet.

The bedchambers were also on this floor, each containing a fireplace and a toilet closet. There is a very good example of this, with some of the original fittings still in place, such as pinewood panelling and a closet.

One of the cupboards originally opened out into a 'press-bed'. The information poster reports that an Englishman visiting Scotland in 1598 wrote: 'their bedsteads were then like cubbards in the wall, with doores to be opened and shut at pleasure'.

The kitchen was built in the 1590s; this was where the food was prepared then cooked over the huge fireplace, while the bread oven was in the corner. There was a stone inlet for water and a trough and drain on the right. A service hatch led through to the passage where food was taken up a stairway to the dining hall above. The remains of the oven can be seen on the outer wall of the castle.

The building combined fine Scottish masonry with the later influence of the classical Renaissance style, apparent in the great hall's fireplace and the detail on some of the doors and windows.

The grounds surrounding the castle are beautifully maintained with a well-kept lawn. In the north-east corner stands a dovecot, part of the earlier construction. At the north side, the castle overlooks the River Clyde with wonderful views across the river to Dumbarton and Cardross.

The one-time owners of the castle, the Maxwell family, had a rather colourful reputation. They were a powerful family with their own share of feuds. The same Patrick who built the 16th century mansion adjoining the castle is reputed to have been involved in murder, but later became a Justice of the Peace.

It is also said that towards the end of his life he ill-treated his wife, causing her to leave him after forty years of marriage and sixteen children. In a plea to the Privy Council, Lady Margaret evidently complained that she 'had charge of his hous quhair in he fund the comfortable efferts of her vertew and industrie.'

Lady Margaret eventually moved to Dumbarton after further cruelty while Sir Patrick ended up being too ill to be brought to trial.

One important event changed the area for ever.

A George Maxwell was involved in merchant shipping between Scotland and the Caribbean and in 1668 he sold some of his Newark acres to the burgesses of Glasgow. They were allowed to erect a port, harbour and other facilities next to the castle, making it easier to trade with Glasgow since the sandbanks on the Clyde prohibited many of the ships from sailing right the way up to Glasgow.

This led to the area being renamed as New-port Glasgow, eventually becoming known as Port Glasgow, as it is today.

The castle passed from the Maxwell family after Sir Patrick died in 1694 and eventually became the property of various people until 1909. Although none of its subsequent owners lived there, the castle did have one or two tenants and the gardens were let to market gardeners.

In the early 1800s, a rope spinner, John Orr, occupied the castle and evidently traded in wild animals from the ships arriving in the harbour.

Now an ancient monument and an 'A' Grade Listed Building looked after by Historic Scotland, Newark Castle is well worth a visit. Unlike other ruins, the castle still retains many of its passages, rooms and narrow, winding stairways and it is very easy to imagine what life in the castle was like from the 15th to 17th centuries.

The visit is enhanced by specially printed colourful drawings and information on the walls of several of the rooms. There is also a well-stocked shop just inside the entrance where the tickets are purchased and modern toilet facilities have been added on the upper floor.

With the mingling of history and shipbuilding still visible in the shipyard and cranes rising just above the castle on its western side, Port Glasgow can be rightly proud of their very own Newark Castle sitting on the shores of the River Clyde.

Published in The Highlander Magazine (USA)

In the Footsteps of Tam o' Shanter

'We think na on the lang Scots miles,
The mosses, waters, slaps and stiles,
That lie between us and our hame,
Where sits our sulky sullen dame,
Gathering her brows like gathering storm,
Nursing her wrath to keep it warm.
This truth fand honest Tam o' Shanter,
As he frae Ayr ae night did canter.'

These lines near the beginning of Robert Burns's famous poem of 1790 set the scene for the tale of Tam o' Shanter, the honest husband who is about to leave the hostelry at Ayr to start the journey home on his faithful grey mare, Maggie (or Meg).

Unfortunately, Tam has been enjoying himself a

bit too much with his great friend, Souter Johnny, by his side and finally leaves the inn late into the evening.

> *'Tam had got planted unco right,*
> *Fast by an ingle, bleezing finely,*
> *Wi' reaming swats, that drank divinely;*
> *And at his elbow, Souter Johnny,*
> *His ancient, trusty, drouthy crony.'*

And so begins Tam's nightmare ride through the countryside of Ayrshire, to reach his waiting wife, Kate, who well knows Tam's predilection for the drink, having warned him about what might happen one of these nights.

> *'She prophesied that late or soon,*
> *Thou would be found, deep drown'd in Doon,*
> *Or catch'd wi' warlocks in the mirk,*
> *By Alloway's auld haunted Kirk.'*

Today, you can still walk among the places mentioned in the tale of Tam o' Shanter. The hostelry is right in the middle of the main street in Ayr and bears a picture of Tam about to mount his faithful mare on the fateful night, with a few lines from the poem on the wall beside it.

Sure enough, some of Kate's warning words were about to come true as Tam finds himself riding through the worst of Scottish weather, with showers, high winds, thunder and lightning. On reaching the auld Kirk at Alloway, Tam sees an astonishing sight.

> *'When, glimmering thro' the groaning trees,*
> *Kirk-Alloway seem'd in a bleeze,*

Thro' ilka bore the beams were glancing,
And loud resounded mirth and dancing.'

Urging his poor mare forward, Tam is determined
to face the very devil to satisfy his curiosity, though
he doesn't really expect to see him. But there in the
midst of the warlocks and witches dancing:

'There sat auld Nick, in shape o' beast;
A towzie tyke, black, grim and large.
To gie them music was his charge.'

Instead of this making Tam turn and ride quickly
for home, he gets more and more caught up in the
skirl of the pipes and the whirling dancers.

Amongst the old crones, one 'winsome wench' in
particular catches his eye: Nannie, in her old Paisley
patterned scanty shirt. Tam is soon mesmerised by the
sight.

'And how Tam stood like ane bewitch'd,
And thought his very een enrich'd.'

Losing all sense of fear and reason, Tam gets
carried away by the moment and, unable to be silent
any longer, he roars out: 'Weel done, Cutty-sark!'
There is an immediate halt to the revelry and Tam
suddenly realises he is now in mortal danger.

'And in an instant all was dark:
And scarcely had he Maggie rallied
When out the hellish legion sallied.'

Although it is now a more modern road than the
country one which Tam would have taken, drive the
couple of miles from Ayr to Alloway today and you

can soon stand in the very churchyard of the ruined auld Kirk where Tam watched the devilish dancers. After reading the poem, it might be best to avoid it by night. This is the same churchyard where Robert Burns's own father is buried. The tombstone also mentions his mother, Agnes Brown, although she was interred in a churchyard in East Lothian.

A pre-reformation church, the auld Kirk was built around 1516, then rebuilt in 1653. It ceased to be used for regular services by the end of the 17th century when the parish was annexed to Ayr.

A little further on you can walk across the same bridge, dating from about the 15th century, which Tam had to flee across for safety. The River Doon still flows beneath it. Although a new bridge was built in 1813, admirers of Burns fortunately managed to prevent the auld brig from being demolished.

Imagine the scene on that dark night, with Tam clutching on to Maggie as the mare flees the churchyard closely followed by the witches. There's only one hope for them both: to reach the bridge over the Doon before the witches reach them.

Tam knows that witches and evil spirits seemingly do not have the power to follow their prey beyond the middle of the next running stream.

> *'Now, do thy speedy utmost, Meg,*
> *And win the key-stane o' the brig;*
> *There at them thou thy tail may toss,*
> *A running stream they darena cross!'*

On they ride, almost at the key stone of the bridge. But Nannie is away ahead of the other witches and makes one last attempt to catch Tam, grabbing at Meg's tail.

The heroic mare keeps on running and Tam escapes the witch's clutches over the Brig o' Doon. But at the cost of Meg's tail, now in the hands of the witch!

Alloway itself is a lovely little village, now home to the Robert Burns Heritage Park. The 70 feet high Burns Monument, situated in the beautiful gardens, was eventually completed in 1823 although the foundation stone was laid on the 25th January 1820, the 61st anniversary of Burns's birth.

Also in the garden is the Statue House where you can see the grinning life-size statues of Tam and his drinking buddy, Johnny Soutar, while Nannie coyly sits away from them. They were carved from single pieces of sandstone by James Thom around the 1830s and, with a little bit of imagination, they bring the characters of the poem to life.

One of Burns's most well-loved poems, Tam and

the terrible loss of his poor mare's tail provides a
salutary *tale* for Burns's readers down through the
ages. Inspired by a local legend of the time, it is
perhaps a warning not to follow too closely in the
footsteps of Tam o' Shanter.

'Now, wha this tale o' truth shall read,
Ilk man and mother's son take heed;
Whene'er to drink you are inclin'd,
Or cutty-sarks run in your mind,
Think! Ye may buy the joys ower dear –
Remember Tam o' Shanter's mare.'

Published in The Highlander Magazine (USA)

James Watt and his Legacy to Greenock

Anyone taking a walk around the main parts of Greenock on the west coast of Scotland, will not fail to be reminded of one of its most famous sons, James Watt, as his name is associated with so many of the town's buildings and historic monuments.

Now that cruise ships visit the town from all parts of the world, this esteemed inventor can be brought to the attention of a new generation of visitors.

Born in Greenock, in January 1736, the young James Watt was mainly taught by his parents, due to ill health, until he eventually went to Grammar School when he was thirteen. He had excellent role models in his grandfather, father and uncle, all of whom were involved in the progression of Greenock as a major shipbuilding area.

Watt's grandfather taught mathematics and navigation in the neighbouring fishing village of Cartsdyke, which eventually became a part of Greenock. His father was apprenticed as a carpenter and shipwright in the 1730s, and subsequently had his own business as a ship owner and merchant. The uncle was a surveyor in Glasgow and produced the first survey of the River Clyde.

With such knowledgeable family members, it is perhaps not surprising that James Watt showed an exceptional mathematical ability by the time he arrived at Grammar School.

By day he added to his learning and satisfied some of his natural curiosity about how things worked, and in the evenings, he put the theory into practise by working in his father's workshop, making models and repairing nautical instruments. The young James was soon to turn such early promise into a world-changing legacy.

By 1755, Watt knew it was time to move on and he went to London in order to serve his apprenticeship as an instrument maker. For most young men, this apprenticeship normally involved three- or four-years training.

James Watt, however, spent only one year training under John Morgan until he had mastered his craft. Then he returned to Scotland.

His first job as a trained instrument maker was at

Glasgow University, where he restored astronomical instruments. By 1757, however, Watt had opened his own shop within the university, proclaiming himself: 'Mathematical Instrument Maker to the University'. It was a measure of his determination to excel at his trade and it gave him the necessary experience to experiment with future projects.

There are probably few people who have not heard of James Watt in relation to the steam engine, but he was not the originator of this new form of power. In 1765, Watt was asked to repair a model of a Newcomen Engine. Since he had already experimented with steam, this was a good chance to learn more. Even more importantly, as it turned out, it allowed Watt to further his own name and career.

Watt repaired the Newcomen Engine model, but he was not entirely satisfied that it worked to the best of its ability. And thus began Watt's own propulsion into history. As he examined the engine and took it to pieces, Watt recognised a fault with it and was sure he knew how to make it much more efficient.

Watt went on to devise an engine with a Separate Condenser which increased its efficiency and overcame the problem of heat loss. This meant that the steam was cooled in a separate chamber. With one port at the top of the cylinder and another at the bottom, each admitted the steam in turn.

As a consequence, the steam entering from below forced the piston up and was then withdrawn. When the port at the top admitted a second charge of steam, this drove the piston down again. It was the beginning of his fame.

In the same year, 1765, Watt was asked to design a pumping engine for a mine at Kinneil. But the project had one problem after another with finance and technical difficulties. Ever the practical innovator, and to earn a wage, Watt turned his hand to civil engineering and surveying work. It was to Greenock's advantage.

Between 1769 and 1774, Watt improved Greenock's harbour and designed the first horse-driven pump that could discharge water from the important dry dock in neighbouring Port Glasgow. During this time, he also constructed two dams that would provide a water supply for Greenock.

Also in 1769, two important events ensured James Watt's place in history. He was granted a patent for his 'New method of lessening the consumption of steam and fuel in fire engines'. He also met Matthew Boulton, an English manufacturer, who was to prove the most beneficial person in the furthering of Watt's career.

Moving to Birmingham in 1774, Watt took the aborted Kinneil engine with him. Since Boulton owned a modern work place with skilled labourers, Watt soon managed to get the Kinneil engine operating satisfactorily. This led to further innovation, when Watt developed his beam engine to allow it to perform a circular motion, which would then drive machinery.

This 'rotary motion', which he patented in 1781, eventually led to many more uses of steam power in such industries as weaving, milling, ceramics, mining and iron works. By 1783, James Watt had set the standard of 'horsepower'.

Meanwhile, the 1780s also saw the prolific James Watt's work on other types of inventions come to fruition.

It may not be so well known that Watt invented a drawing machine and two unique printing presses: a screw down press and a roller press. These could reproduce technical letters and drawings onto semi-transparent paper from an inked original. He patented these in 1780 and a model of his portable copying press is in the Mclean Museum in Greenock, adjacent to the Watt Library.

Watt's illustrious career came to an end in 1800, when his original patent expired, and he retired. But his invention was to lead the great shipbuilding town of Greenock well into the next century.

Since other engineers were now allowed to experiment on Watt's designs, it led to the building of the *Comet*, the first seagoing commercial steamboat in Europe, which was built by John Wood of Port Glasgow in 1812. Two years on, the Boulton and Watt engines were used in the *Prince of Orange* and the *Princess Charlotte*, both built by James Munn of Greenock.

James Watt's legacy to Greenock has been immortalised for future generations. In 1816, Watt donated £100 to the magistrates of Greenock in order to set up a Scientific Library. He stipulated that the books must cover subjects from the properties of fluids to shipbuilding.

When Watt died in 1819, the people of Greenock commissioned a marble statue of James Watt, by Sir Francis Chantrey. Watt's son provided a building to house the statue along with the collections of the Greenock Library. With the site donated by the Shaw Stewart family, the Watt Library opened in 1837. The adjoining museum and Watt Hall were added in 1876.

The Watt Library now contains a magnificent collection of local history, archives and genealogy as well as general books. A Watt Memorial College was opened in 1908, in the area where Watt had lived as a child.

Not surprisingly, the main subjects taught were marine engineering and navigation. This original college closed in 1973, when a new James Watt College opened. Today, a further Waterfront Campus has been opened, ensuring the continuation of Watt's legacy to learning, although a broad range of subjects was long ago added to the original on offer.

In addition to the once acclaimed James Watt Dock, two other monuments remind Greenock people of the town's famous inventor. On the main road through the town, there is an impressive statue of James Watt which was erected on the site of his birthplace.

The other is the Watt Cairn in Greenock cemetery, which is a lasting memorial to his genius throughout the world. The plaque on the Cairn reads:

PROJECTED AND COMMENCED
BY THE WATT CLUB 1854
ARRANGED AND COMPLETED ON THE
200TH ANNIVERSARY OF WATT'S BIRTH, 1936.
THESE STONES, GIFTED FROM
ALL PARTS OF THE WORLD,
SPEAK OF THE UNIVERSAL HOMAGE
ACCORDED THE GREAT
ENGINEER, INVENTOR AND SCIENTIST.
THE MONUMENT ALSO MARKS THE BURYING
PLACE OF JAMES WATT'S ANCESTORS
REMOVED FROM THE OLD WEST KIRK, 1922

Although it was one of the leading shipbuilding towns in Scotland from the 19th century, Greenock and the neighbouring towns on either side, Port Glasgow and Gourock, really began to thrive and grow because of Watt's application of steam power to navigation and the building of iron steam ships.

With almost a quarter of Britain's sugar refineries in Greenock and Port Glasgow at one time, not to mention the textile mills and the Clyde steamers, James Watt's legacy went far beyond the invention of the Separate Condenser and the modification to that original Newcomen engine.

Published in The Highlander Magazine (USA)

Dunfermline Abbey in Fife

Dunfermline Abbey is an impressive sight with its tall, square tower on which the name of King Robert the Bruce is carved in stone on its four sides.

A Benedictine Abbey was founded by Queen Margaret on the site in the 11th century but all that remains are the foundations under the nave of what is now called the 'Old Church', which was built in the 12th century. Adjoining the original church is the 19th century Abbey Church which is still used for services today.

Dedicated in 1147, little remains inside the old church apart from its massive pillars, beautiful stained-glass windows and the 'Old Nave', although there is some fine carving around the outside of the south door. Of the five pillars on the left and six on the right, one pillar on each side has an interesting chevron pattern. A gallery runs the whole length of the building to either side.

One of the stained-glass windows depicts the Coat of Arms of the mother of King James I of Scotland, Queen Anabella Drummond, consort of Robert III. Only a fragment of the great rood, or cross, has survived at the eastern end of the nave, before the entrance to the more modern church.

There is quite a contrast going from the old church to the new, especially in the light and brightness of the interior. Many features of historic interest remain, as well as stunning stained-glass windows, such as the McLaren Window of 1904 above the pulpit. The lower half of this window depicts the Last Supper.

One of the most attractive features of this church is the richly carved wood. The pulpit, from 1890, is most striking and the Abbey Guide suggests "it is one of the finest of its kind in Scotland." It was carved by William Paterson and gifted to the church by the Earl of Elgin and Kincardineshire.

Each of the four Evangelists is carved at one of the corners and is depicted with his personal symbol: Matthew, the Lion of Judah; Mark, the simplest of men; Luke, the ox of sacrifice; John, the eagle of vision. There are individual circles representing the twelve disciples. Other intricate carving depicts the Passion of Christ.

The exquisite lectern was carved by Thomas Good in 1931 and was a direct result of a visit by Queen Mary when she noticed there was no lectern. The present-day organ is an amalgamation of periods. A four-manual organ was built in 1911 and partly incorporated the original 1880s two-manual organ.

Then, in 1967, the organ was again rebuilt, reducing it to a three-manual instrument.

The most extensive work was carried out between 1984 and 1986, when the organ was completely removed during structural renovation of the Abbey.

The internal layout of the organ was redesigned and refined to a high standard. Containing around 3000 pipes, it is one of the finest in the country.

Not only is the name of King Robert the Bruce carved on the four sides of the Abbey tower, his tomb is situated directly beneath the pulpit inside the church.

Originally buried in Dunfermline Abbey in 1329, the exact spot was unknown for centuries. In 1818, workmen discovered the vault containing the King's remains.

This was verified when official inspection showed that the breastbone was severed to allow the heart to be taken to the holy land according to the Bruce's wishes.

The remains were ceremoniously re-interred between the transepts, and the magnificent medieval-type brass embedded in marble was made in 1889 to cover the tomb.

The translated Latin inscription reads: "The tomb of Robert the Bruce, King of Scots, fortunately discovered among the ruins in 1818, has been anew marked by this brass in the 560th year after his death."

During the 700th anniversary of his death, in 1974, a new stained-glass window, the Bruce Memorial Window, was installed in the north transept and dedicated to the king's memory.

There are several marble monuments to the Bruce family in the south transept, including a General whose illness in the Holy land was tended by the then Prince of Wales, the future Edward VII.

The beautiful Memorial Chapel was set apart in memory of those members who died in action during the two World Wars. Every item placed in the chapel has been donated in memory of someone.

The congregation gifted a Royal Pew to the chapel in 1972, especially for Queen Elizabeth II and Prince Philip when they attended a special service to mark the 900th anniversary of the founding of the Abbey.

There is an impressive list of all the Royals who are buried in Dunfermline Abbey plus eight Armorial Banners with full details.

Volunteer Guides are usually available to visitors and written information is provided at various points.

Dumbarton: Castle on the Rock

From the M8 motorway, across on the other side of the River Clyde, it looks like a strange rock-like hill looming out from the water's edge. But look closer and you will see that the rock is almost divided in two, with an old mansion, battlements and canons nestling in between the two peaks.

Examine it even closer and you will discover that many steps lead up to the top of the rock where, along with the panoramic views down the Clyde, there are the remains of a French Prison. This rock, Dumbarton Castle, was the ancient royal seat of the once independent kingdom of Strathclyde.

The Rock is in fact a plug of volcanic basalt jutting from the river but one with interesting fortifications, added to until the eighteenth century. The original name, *Dun Breatann*, means 'the fortress of the Britons', although it had an even older name in the Dark Ages: *Alcluith* appropriately meaning 'Clyde Rock'.

This was a precarious time of raids and sieges, with Strathclyde in the middle of powerful kingdoms on all sides, such as Northumbria, Picts and Dalriadic Scots, as well as being plundered by the Vikings from Ireland. Then, in 1018, Malcolm II's son, Duncan, took the throne of Strathclyde and governed Dumbarton until it finally became part of the Scottish Kingdom in 1034.

Dumbarton Castle had a chequered history right up until the nineteenth century and, considering its humble appearance, it played host to many of Scotland's famous people. Because of its strategic position on the river, Dumbarton was a stronghold and entry port for the west of Scotland but it was also a royal castle as proved by a charter of 1238, which was given to the Earl of Lennox, the local magnate.

The castle soon caught the interest of Edward I who appointed the governor Sir John Menteith to keep it under his control. This was the Menteith who was subsequently involved in the capture of William Wallace in 1305 and many assume that the famous freedom fighter may have been kept at the castle at some point, although this has never been confirmed.

The relative seclusion of Dumbarton Castle leant itself well to some of the intrigue prevalent in Scotland at the time. It offered protection to many a royal, such as King David II who, after a Scottish defeat, later sailed to France with his consort, Joan.

During the fifteenth century, this small fortress was under siege time and again. Used as a bargaining tool by Walter de Danyelstone, who hoped to be appointed bishop of St Andrews, it was then seized by a Patrick Galbraith who took the castle in 1443 after killing the keeper.

Then it was James IV's turn. He first attacked in 1489 when the castle was controlled by Lord Darnley, son of the earl of Lennox, but it was only after his second attack that James forced the surrender. He quickly realised that the castle's situation on the water's edge was perfect as a shipbuilding base for his new navy, from whence he sailed to western parts of the country.

The castle's relative peace was soon destroyed once more when James IV was killed at Flodden. Through much of the sixteenth century, it passed from one person to another, between English and French allegiance, even playing host to the infant Mary Stewart, Queen of Scots, in 1548 when she was brought to the castle some months before being taken to France.

Despite further changes of hand, the castle was held for Mary after her return to Scotland, until her final flight to England in 1568, accompanied by the governor of Dumbarton, Lord Fleming.

Once again, the castle's relative calm was short-lived, with two more attempts to seize it. This culminated in the execution of one of Mary's main adherents, John Hamilton, the archbishop of St Andrews. Dumbarton Castle was now no longer a stronghold for Mary, Queen of Scots.

During the greater part of the seventeenth century, the castle once more was a place of dispute, as indeed was much of the country in those days of Covenanters and Royalists. During the 'Bishop's War' of 1639, the Covenanters managed to capture the governor while he was at church and insisted he surrender the keys. This time, an official document, The Treaty of Berwick, ensured that the castle was returned to the Royalists. It seemed to make little difference in the end, as the castle changed hands twice more inside two years!

Unsurprisingly, all these sieges and skirmishes left their mark on the castle and grounds, continuing over the next century. Once General Cromwell took control of Scotland, Dumbarton Castle soon followed in 1652. However, even then, its disrepair and change of hands continued as before, when it was retaken by a Royalist raid in 1654.

The following hundred years saw the castle in somewhat poorer condition, although certain improvements were gradually made. By the 1790s, the country was in the midst of the French wars and the castle was duly made ready once more to defend the Scottish coast. However, it was not to last and the castle was largely abandoned in 1865, only being used eventually by the military during World Wars I and II.

With so many hundred years of occupation and attack, it is not surprising that few of the castle's original features survive, although there is the odd piece of evidence to prove its long heritage. There are, however, several interesting features from the eighteenth century which makes it well worth a visit. Many of them are visible from the pleasant gardens at the edge of the river.

Entry to the castle grounds is up a short flight of steps and through the eighteenth-century outer gate. A glance to the left at this point reveals the circular domed sentinel box of King George's Battery which juts out from this part of the castle wall and is one of the main focal points from the surrounding area. However, it is the imposing Governor's House, built in 1735, that commands attention. The upper part is still occupied but visitors are welcome to explore the artefacts in the museum on the lower floor.

Behind the mansion house, a long flight of stone steps leads to the upper parts of the Rock. But first you must pass through the sixteenth century Guard House. Inside are the two oldest remains found in the area; gravestones from about the tenth or eleventh century, which were excavated in one of the garden terraces. Through the other side of the Guard House, the steps continue upwards, passing under the fourteenth century Portcullis Arch, which is thought to be the oldest structure surviving on the Rock.

At one time, this would have blocked access to the flat area between the two summits, although it was also used as a bridge between them at times. It is a long steep walk to the top of Dumbarton Castle but it is worth persevering, not least for the views up and down the River Clyde, while the River Leven can be seen from the western side.

There are two directions in which to walk from the Portcullis Arch: to the western summit, White Tower Craig, where there is nothing more exciting than the remains of an eighteenth-century windmill, or north to the level centre between the summits.

The latter was the centre of occupation throughout the Rock's history but the only surviving building is the 18th century French Prison used during the Napoleonic wars, which is now undergoing some renovation.

There was another point of entry to the castle at one time, the North Entry, which faced the town of Dumbarton. It was through here that the Earl of Lennox sneaked under the gate and captured the castle in 1514. However, this entrance was soon a ruin and was eventually incorporated into the Duke of York's Battery at the end of the 18th century.

One other interesting building remains on the eastern summit: The Magazine, which contained one hundred and fifty barrels of powder and was built on the Beak in 1748 to withstand any gunfire or artillery bombs. There are a few more batteries at strategic points around the Rock, although none as impressive as the black cannons that forever aim towards the Clyde from King George's Battery in front of the Governor's House.

Dumbarton Castle is now in the care of Historic Scotland and some of its remaining structures are under renovation. It is a hidden gem, nestling on its twin-peaked volcanic rock. Yet, it is questionable how many people viewing it from across the water would ever believe that such an unassuming rock was once at the very centre of Scotland's turbulent history.

As Dorothy Wordsworth, said of Dumbarton Castle in 1803:

*"I never saw rock in nobler masses, or more deeply
stained by time and weather; nor is this to be
wondered at, for it is in the very eye of
sea-storms and land-storms, of mountain winds
and water winds."*

A Day in Inveraray Jail

If you have ever wondered what prison life was like in nineteenth century Scotland, a day in Inveraray Jail is the place to be, for it recreates the experience in an almost too realistic way. To add to the illusion, a man and woman in authentic nineteenth century dress play the part of various characters at the most unexpected times.

Comprising the Courtroom, Old Prison, New Prison and Airing Yards, the old Inveraray Jail was completely restored and reopened to the public in May 1989; almost 100 years after the last prisoner left its confines. A visit 'inside' gives a real sense of the conditions experienced by those nineteenth century men, women and children unlucky enough to have been detained within its cells.

Between the building of the Old Prison in 1820 and the New Prison in 1848, many reforms were taking place and this is evident in the different conditions the prisoners faced.

Entrance to the Jail is by way of the imposing Courthouse built between 1816 and 1820. The spacious Courtroom was used for three different types of court sittings: Circuit Court, Sheriff Court and Burgh Court, as well as various meetings.

It is a disquieting experience today, to walk into what appears to be the middle of a trial. The Courtroom is set out exactly as it would have been during a Circuit Court Session around 1850. A fifteen-man jury sits to one side, witnesses on the other, while the lawyers sit below the judge. The accused sits in the dock facing the lawyers and judge.

At the beginning of the trial, the members of the jury were called one by one by the Clerk of the Court to stand in the jury box while the following oath was administered:

"You fifteen swear by Almighty God and as you will answer to God on the Great Day of Judgement, that you will truth say and no truth conceal, so far as you are to pass at this assize."

It is spookily life-like in the courtroom and, to add to the effect, visitors are encouraged to sit in the public benches to listen to extracts from real trials. It doesn't take much imagination to believe you are indeed sitting in the middle of a nineteenth century trial. In fact, the judge's wife sitting in the VIP seat, in her red bonnet and dress, seemed remarkably real and, although she was perfectly still, I was convinced she was breathing.

The exit from the courtroom leads to the beautifully restored Old Prison, completed in 1820.

This was the main county jail for the whole of Argyll and a ghastly place it must have been; surely a powerful deterrent against any thought of re-offending! Comprising eight small cells, this prison held men, women, children, sane and insane often crowded together.

One can only imagine the horrors for, in the earliest years, there was little ventilation or heating, no hope of exercise or occupation and, unbelievably, no washroom or water closet. Petty criminals might share space with murderers, the convicted with the yet to be convicted.

There is a taste of the dark and dreadful conditions in the realistic exhibition of prisoners locked in their cells. When the 'matron' suddenly appeared and ordered me to prison, it took a moment for the shock to subside and to remember this was only a portrayal of how it used to be.

Although these conditions lasted for over ten years in Inveraray, and elsewhere in Scotland, prison reformers finally succeeded in making a difference.

The Prisons Act of 1835 and the Prisons Scotland Act of 1839 led to much needed rules for the more humane care of prisoners and proper training for prison staff. Cells had to be bigger, with daylight, ventilation and heat, while prisoners were to be clothed, fed and exercised.

Many changes were put into effect at once, but it was eight years before a new prison was completed. Meanwhile, airing yards were constructed in 1843 to allow the prisoners to exercise for an hour each day in the fresh air. Considering the typical wet Scottish weather, it was as well they were provided with capes when necessary. However, it was a step forward in allowing prisoners much needed air and exercise.

The airing yards remained until 1882, then for the next seven years all the prisoners were exercised together in the prison yards.

The New Prison, finally completed in 1848, was a model prison of its time. As opposed to the eight cells in the overcrowded Old Prison, the new one had twelve individual cells, a water closet on each floor, washroom, accommodation for warders and an exercise gallery. Lit by gas, it also had adequate heating and ventilation

From 1839, physically fit prisoners were expected to work in their cells for up to ten hours a day which included making herring nets, picking oakum (fibre from old rope), shoemaking, tailoring, joinery, knitting and sewing.

It wasn't an option whether to work or not, as there was punishment for under achieving their quota. However, as well as providing some occupation, it also allowed hard workers to receive a small payment for any extra work. This was given to them on the day they left prison.

For all the reforms that made prison life more bearable, some authorities decided it had become too easy in the 1850s. Instead of the usual hammock, mattress, blankets, sheets and pillow, unfortunate prisoners now had to endure a wooden guard bed and wooden pillows for the first thirty days of their sentence!

However, it wasn't only the prisoners who had a tough time. The life of the prison governor, and often his wife, was a hard one. Expected to work seven days a week, he was responsible for checking on each male prisoner every day and female prisoners once a week, accompanied by his wife who looked after the women.

As well as conducting periodic searches of the prison, the governor had to keep records and a journal, while returning regular reports and generally turning his hand to anything else that might be required.

The only other help they had was from the warder. This unfortunate man had to sleep in the prison and work long hours for little payment. No wonder a suitable candidate was difficult to find, for the warder must be of exemplary character, and sober at all times: "Swearing and improper language, frequenting public houses, keeping bad company were grounds for dismissal."

Once Inveraray Jail closed to prisoners on 31st August 1889, the county police took it over as a short-term detention centre. Gradually, however, the Circuit Court moved to Oban and the Sheriff Court to Dunoon in 1954, causing the jail to fall into disrepair.

The Scottish Office is to be congratulated for

restoring this beautiful nineteenth century building, for it is indeed a step back in time to spend a day in Inveraray Jail. I was very thankful, however, to be only a visitor!

House for an Abbot

Although it stands in the shadow of Dunfermline Abbey, the authentic salmon pink façade of the 15th and 16th century Abbot House ensures it has always been one of the most visited tourist attractions in the historic town of Dunfermline in Fife, one-time capital of Scotland and original burial place of Scotland's Kings and Queens.

A beautiful building by any standards, as well as the oldest house in Dunfermline, Abbot House is a heritage centre where the well set-out displays in the upper rooms provide a step back through thousands of years of Scottish history.

But first, it is worth having a cup of tea or coffee in one of the original barrel-vaulted rooms on the ground floor. While enjoying the excellent home baking provided and served by volunteers, it is a good way to get a feeling for the past.

Some of these rooms have iron sculptures of the tools used long ago. In one, there is a baking griddle to denote the kitchen, and the doors leading out to the garden have little wrought iron figurines of the appropriate trade: bakers with chef hats.

A restored stained-glass panel on one wall illustrates a scene from *The Ballad of Sir Patrick Spens*, an old Scottish song that seemingly tells the story of the ill-fated voyage of Margaret, Maid of Norway, across the sea from Norway to Scotland.

The lintel above the fireplace is inscribed with a quotation from the first verse in its original language:

> *"The King sits in Dunfermling Toune*
> *Drinking the blude reid wine*
> *O whaur will I get a guid sailor*
> *Tae sail this schip o mine."*

The seal of another Patrick, the 5th Abbot of Dunfermline in the 13th century, is on the opposite wall and is now the emblem of Abbot House, as depicted on the sign hanging over the entrance.

Another of the white-washed vaulted rooms shows decorative hammers and blacksmith's aprons on the doors, leading to the conclusion that this may once have been an iron forge as well as a bakery. This is further suggested by the *swey* in the fireplace that would have suspended a pot over the flames.

One room, built around 1660 and outside the main 15th century wall of the house, is named The Fire Room. This is thought to have replaced the original gallery which was probably damaged in the Great Fire of Dunfermline in 1624. Part of the original floor is now visible and the artist, David Wilkinson, has painted scenes around the room depicting the possible view from Abbot House on the day of the fire.

The terrible event itself was seemingly started when a young lad fired a musket at pigeons on a thatched roof where it caught fire and destroyed around two thirds of the town's houses. Abbot House and Dunfermline Abbey survived due to being built of stone.

On payment of a small fee, visitors are allowed to explore the upper rooms and displays, with the option of being accompanied by a knowledgeable guide. However, the real story of Abbot House begins with a visit to the audio-visual presentation, 'The Spirit in the Stones', to hear the friendly ghost recount the house's history.

It is a history of Scotland's past and each of the rooms in the house depicts a particular era, from the Picts through to a replica 1960s room, with Kings and

Queens and various interesting Scottish figures in between.

It is also fun to look out for the variety of distinctive stone mason's marks throughout the building, particularly along the first-floor passage. With all the different construction on the House over the last five hundred years, there is always something new being discovered about its past.

While ascending the spiral staircase of the West Tower, visitors can see a phrase carved on the fireplace lintel above the doorway; also seen above the entrance doorway.

This quotation is from the 15th century work by James I of Scotland, *The Kingis Quair*, and is thought have been put there after the Reformation of 1560 to ensure that matters discussed inside the walls remained private:

SEN VORD IS THRALL AND THOCHT IS FRE
KEIP VEILL THY TONGE I COINSELL THE

This is loosely translated as: "*Since word is binding but thought is transient, think what you like but don't say it.*"

Abbot House is filled with much memorabilia relating to Queen Margaret, wife of King Malcolm III and mother of three subsequent Scottish Kings. One of the most colourful and interesting rooms on the first floor is that dedicated to Margaret who was canonised in 1249 to become known as Saint Margaret.

This room is decorated in medieval style, to portray how Dunfermline Abbey might have looked before the reformation. There are three paintings in this room: St Margaret, the Holy Trinity and St Andrew, all executed in vibrant 13th century colour by artist, Virginia Colley.

In her left hand, Saint Margaret is holding her *Gospel Book*, which had miraculously survived immersion in running water, while *The Holy Rood Cross* is in her right hand. This was an important symbol of power of the Church in Scotland and was seized with the Stone of Scone by Edward 1 in 1291.

Also in this room is a replica of the jewel-encrusted headshrine which would have contained St Margaret's skull. This was known as a portable reliquary and the fate of the original is unknown. This gorgeous replica is silver with a gold crown and among the jewels are pearls, depicting the name Margaret which means pearl. A crystal on the breast would have allowed glimpses of the Saint's hair.

There is also an example of a chained library, of the type once found in Dunfermline Abbey, where the precious volumes were protected from robbers by being chained to the shelves. In one corner is the figure of a kneeling monk, John Boiswell, a sacristan in the Abbey who went on to buy Abbot House in 1540, once it had been vacated by the previous Abbot.

Further along this floor is the fascinating Lady Halkett's Room, decorated and furnished in the style of her private study. It is believed that this room is outside the original front wall of the House and was built around 1660 to replace the gallery that once existed at this level. Part of the ceiling has been removed to allow visitors to see some of the tower staircase and wooden guttering with original metal brackets.

Formerly Anne Murray, daughter of Charles I's tutor, Lady Halkett was a Jacobite supporter and eventually left the Court in London to settle in Scotland. She had a colourful life before she met and married the widowed Sir James Halkett.

On his death, her stepson forced her to leave his father's estate, but she was kindly offered use of Abbot House by the Seton family and she stayed there until her death in 1699. She never gave up her Jacobite sympathies and ran a residential school for the supporters' sons in Abbot House, while providing a soup kitchen and herb clinic for the poor. A pious woman in those days, Lady Anne wrote religious tracts and many diaries which are now portrayed in her room in the House.

Other very interesting rooms include The Presence Chamber, where important visitors to Dunfermline Abbey would have been received by the Abbot and where all the Abbey's business would have been carried out. As well as the two fireplaces, the most exciting discovery in this room was the quatrefoil traceried window which was then dated from 1450-1460, along with the north wall of the Abbot House.

This was of great importance as it proved the House existed before the Reformation and the rebuilt house of 1571. The room contains the figure of lawyer, schoolmaster and medieval poet, Robert Henryson writing at his desk, while murals of his best-known work have been painted around the walls.

The next room, The Marbled Chamber, depicts the period following the Restoration of the Monarchy of 1660 and in pride of place is the Crown Chair. The cushions were embroidered by a National Trust for Scotland group, with a mathematical pattern thought to be in memory of John Napier, inventor of natural logarithms. Among the display cabinets is one containing a replica sword belonging to King Robert the Bruce.

Further interesting rooms are: The Reform Room, portraying the living area of a family from the late 18th century, with authentic furnishings and artefacts; The War Room, decorated in 1941 when used as Headquarters for the 1145 Squadron of the Air Training Corps; The Industrial Room, built around 1660 and dedicated to the industries once thriving Fife such as coal, brick and fireclay works, with the essential time clock that allowed employees to 'clock in' and clock out' each day.

The Entertainment Room is decorated in 1920s-40s Art Deco style, providing the nostalgia of theatre, cinema and Opera House, with programmes and sheet music. The final room is decorated in the style of the 1960s, complete with authentic living room furniture and television. This was chosen as the cut-off date of the displays, to coincide with the opening of the Forth Road Bridge in 1964.

Among the other points of interest is The Long Gallery which is full of fascinating detail and includes a seated statue of one of Dunfermline's famous sons, Andrew Carnegie, who was born in the town in 1835. Most visitors love to be photographed sitting beside this remarkable philanthropist.

Of further interest is the statue of Anna Munro, the suffragette and Scottish Organiser of the Women's Freedom League in 1909, who proudly stands in front of posters declaring Votes for Women.

There is so much of interest inside Abbot House that one visit is never enough and new discoveries are always being made. There is a very good guide book available from the shop giving much more information, but nothing takes the place of wandering around examining each item and every uncovered wall or floor, for the building itself speaks of its colourful past.

Even the grounds of Abbot House are interesting, from the beautiful scented gardens with sundial and Spirit of Eternity Fountain, to the wrought-iron gates covered with intricate iron figures. Then there is the Wallace Plaque on the garden's side wall depicting the figure of a woman with baby and child, with the legend:

> *'Margaret mother of William Wallace lies buried*
> *beneath a thorn tree*
> *in the grounds of Dunfermline Abbey'.*

There is the inescapable knowledge that this place is full of centuries of Scottish history. And if you are lucky, the resident peacock from the nearby Pittencrieff Park might grace the gardens with his presence.

No matter how many visits are made to Abbot House, each time there is yet another fascinating fact or piece of original structure displayed, and no doubt many are still waiting to be uncovered.

It is indeed a house fit for an Abbot in this ancient town of Scottish monarchy.

Abbot House is currently awaiting re-opening after changing hands

Inchmahome: Priory on the Lake

Hidden away in the centre of the only lake in Scotland (all others are called lochs), Inchmahome Priory is a delightfully secluded piece of history reached only by a small boat. The crossing takes a mere eight minutes but anticipation builds as the boat slows down on approach to the short pier.

Situated on one of the three islands on the Lake of Menteith in the west of Scotland, the ruins of the priory gradually reveal themselves to visitors as the peaceful ambience takes hold.

No matter how busy the island becomes in the height of summer, there is a strange sense of being apart from the world, almost as though the spirituality of its past surrounds present day trippers.

Dating from 1238, Inchmahome Priory was founded by Walter Comyn, the 13th century Earl of Menteith, as a spiritual retreat for the local Augustinian order and all connected to them. Permission was finally granted by the Bishop of Dunblane after a lengthy dispute and an eventual authorisation from Pope Gregory IX.

Although most of the original buildings are now in ruins, apart from the chapter house, enough remains to offer a real sense of their use. In addition to the details provided on plaques around the ruins, the official Historic Scotland guide adds plenty of colour and information to bring the past to life.

One of the signs includes a quote from the original authorisation permitting Walter Comyn to build the priory: "It shall be lawful for the said earl and his successors to build a house for religious men of the order of St Augustine, in the island of Inchmaquhomok."

The priory evidently replaced an even older parish church and it soon became the holy centre of all activity on the island, often welcoming local parishioners to worship in the nave, including the earl and countess of Menteith and their household from the nearby island of Inch Talla.

After alighting from the boat, the ruins of the main priory church are immediately visible, with many of the impressively carved Gothic arches still intact. Once the heart of priory life, it is still possible to gain an idea of the majesty of the once enclosed building.

The published guide suggests that scenes from the Bible may have adorned the brightly painted walls. It is easy to imagine the various statues that would have stood in narrow niches, or the candles providing extra light to mingle with the sun streaming through stained-glass windows.

In common with many large churches of the period, a rood screen or cross would have divided the choir, where the canons gathered for worship, from the nave. One of the most interesting features still visible is the sedilia: the three seats occupied by the priest and his assistants during a mass. Evidently among the earliest to survive in Scotland, they afford the modern visitor a tangible link to the past.

A little further along the wall, stood the basin, or piscine, where the priest washed his hands and the sacred vessels during the service, the water draining to the ground outside the church. A small cupboard, known as an aumbry, hid the consecrated Host and crucifix until required on Easter day.

As in many monasteries, cloisters at Inchmahome Priory would once have provided a quiet garden area for reading and contemplation. Most of the priory's domestic buildings were arranged around the cloisters and some of the ruins still provide an indication of their use, although only a few stone steps reveal the addition of an upper floor at one time.

One of the most interesting buildings on the island, and the only one still roofed, is the chapter house, second only to the church in importance. This was where the canons met each day to discuss the business and other important matters such as discipline, as well as to hear readings from the Rule of St Augustine.

The distinctive pitched roof was added in the 17th century, when the chapter house was converted into a mausoleum and it is one of the most atmospheric places on the island. Surrounded by ruins and an impression of the past, this building provides memorial items from long-ago history.

Stepping inside the chapter house immediately draws the visitor into a previous age, enhanced by the opportunity to sit on the same cold stone benches set around the room, where priests of old held council. The arched, stained-glass window adds to the sense of the past while the fragments of carved ancient grave slabs depict historical figures and Celtic designs.

But most awe-inspiring of all is the touching

effigy of Walter Stewart, who died in 1295, eternally entwined with that of his countess, Mary. Another effigy is that of an armed knight, the shield emblazoned with the Stewart arms. Sitting in such a peaceful memorial, it is only a short stretch of the imagination to hear the voices of long-gone Augustinian canons.

The other domestic buildings are less discernible from what is left of the ruins but there is the suggestion of at least a kitchen, warming house and latrine. The remaining steps of a staircase would have led up to the upper floor and a dormitory. The discovery of around thirty human skulls in the 1930s indicated the situation of an infirmary as part of the priory, which was in keeping with most monastic orders.

The daily life of the dozen or so canons on Inchmahome was largely spent in silence, apart from periods of prayer and choral singing, or at other specific times. As Augustinian canons, they followed the Rule of St Augustine, the oldest monastic rule in western lands, dating from the year 430.

Although worship, prayer and the work of God was their primary purpose, with the days divided into several church services, they also had periods for reading, studying and a little manual work such as gardening or fishing.

Inchmahome Island played host to a royal visitor in 1547. Four-year-old Mary Queen of Scots was taken there by her mother, dowager Queen Marie de Guise, for sanctuary after the Scots were defeated at the Battle of Pinkie. Not only was it near enough to Stirling, but the island was also under the control of Mary's guardian, Lord Erskine.

Although her stay lasted only three weeks, and the

following year she was taken to France, her visit was commemorated by naming a boxwood enclosed area in the centre of the island Queen Mary's Bower. Robert the Bruce was another famous name who visited Inchmahome three times in the early 1300s during the Scottish Wars of Independence.

By the time the Protestant Reformation took hold in Scotland in 1560, and Inchmahome Priory was abandoned, it had already undergone other changes with the royal appointment of Robert, Master of Erskine, as head of the priory in 1529.

When the Graham family acquired Inchmahome and neighbouring Inch Talla in the 1600s, they not only planted trees and gardens but they also transformed the chapter house into a large mausoleum. However, the avenue and gate they added were removed by the State in the 1920s and the chapter house somewhat restored to its original.

Inchmahome is still a remarkably peaceful island of natural beauty considering the number of visitors it receives, with plentiful trees, paths, wildlife and beautiful scenery around the tranquil lake.

But step into the centre of the ruins or sit in the dim light of the chapter house, and the echoes of the past seem very near, as though a church bell is about to ring to summon the canons to their worship.

As the boat carries the day trippers back to modern life, Inchmahome Priory will no doubt draw them again one day to the peaceful embrace of another life and time on this Island of Rest.

Published in The Highlander Magazine (USA)

Steamship Sir Walter Scott, Loch Katrine

Loch Katrine was mentioned by the famous Scottish writer Sir Walter Scott, in his *Lady of the Lake* poem of 1810 and modern visitors can still sail on the steamship bearing his name.

The Sir Walter Scott steamer has been sailing on Loch Katrine for over 100 years and still continues to offer visitors a gentle cruise along the tranquil water. There is no more peaceful way to enjoy the scenery, with the backdrop of green hills typical of this lovely part of Scotland.

The author described the view in his poem as: "The summer dawns, reflected hue, the purple changed Loch Katrine blue." It is exactly the same today, as the steamship begins its sails from the wooden Trossachs Pier at the foot of the loch.

Loch Katrine is situated in Scotland's first National Park, near Callander and Aberfoyle. Its name means a highland robber, from the Gaelic 'Cateran' and it is right in the heart of Clan MacGregor country.

The most famous member of the clan was Rob Roy MacGregor whose birthplace, Glengyle, is at the head of the loch. He has often been immortalised in print and film as a kind of highland hero. Rob Roy was born near the end of the Scottish Clan system and had opposed the titled, powerful land owners and law makers who finally dismantled the old ways.

The water in the loch is very pure and has been the source of the water supply for the city of Glasgow since 1859. It is still fed by the crystal-clear mountain streams as it was in Victorian times when the steamer first sailed. The loch is almost ten miles long and just over one-mile wide and the steamship sails as far as Stronachlachar. A sail on the steamship is the perfect way to admire the stunning scenery, with majestic mountains, small islands, woodland and wildlife.

Built by Wm Denny and Bros Ltd at Dumbarton on the River Clyde, the little steamship was launched in 1899. It is the last screw-driven steamship still in service on Scottish inland waters. Usually there is a crew of five on board: the captain, mate, engineer, stoker and deckhand, and the ship is licensed to carry 320 passengers.

The steamship still retains the original steam engine which runs on smokeless fuel which is necessary to maintain the purity of the water in the loch. There would be too much danger of oil spillage if it were ever converted to diesel, which would be an unthinkable risk to the loch which ultimately supplies water to Glasgow.

In addition to the famous steamship, Loch Katrine is an ideal venue for walkers and cyclists with a picturesque, quiet road winding its way right up the northern side of the loch. There are viewpoints at strategic points on the route to enjoy the scenery or watch out for the steamship chugging up the loch. Picnic areas make it a great day out. For those wanting more exercise, there is a climb to the top of Ben A'an (about 1488 feet) where the reward is the beauty of the surrounding view.

Visitors can bring their own bicycles but there is also cycle hire available at Katrinewheelz, where there is a great variety of bikes to suit everyone. As an alternative to picnics, the Anchor's Rest offers coffees and meals overlooking the stunning loch and hills.

The Steamship Sir Walter Scott runs every day from May through to October. There is a comfortable lounge, toilet and refreshments onboard and a member of the crew gives an interesting commentary on the area, as the ship gently sails along the loch.

Strathspey Railway, Aviemore

Setting off from the popular skiing resort of Aviemore, the Strathspey Railway is a round trip of about one and a half hours through the Scottish countryside.

The Strathspey Railway offers a nostalgic train journey from Aviemore to Boat of Garten and on to Broomhill. Run almost completely by enthusiastic volunteers, it is a comfortable, relaxing way to enjoy the glorious Scottish scenery the way visitors did in the more leisurely days of steam.

During the 19th century, Aviemore, on the banks of the River Spey, was developed as a railway junction after the main line to Inverness was completed in 1898.

The railway was essential for the economy of the area by the late 1800s. As well as bringing goods to the highland area, it allowed the transport of Scottish timber.

During the First World War, the Canadian Forestry Corps helped to fell trees in the area and they built their own 3'0" gauge railway line which ran from the woods into the loading bank at Aviemore Station.

When the main line route to Forres closed in 1965, Aviemore was no longer required as a railway junction and, as a consequence, the trains stopped running.

Aviemore soon became a leading winter sports centre, offering visitors a good range of restaurants, shops and leisure facilities, including excellent skiing in the Cairngorms. Since tourism was the biggest source of income to the town, it was the main reason that the old railway line was eventually reopened.

By 1978, the Strathspey Railway opened between Speyside Station, on the outskirts of Aviemore, and Boat of Garten. Aviemore itself suffered a halt to its tourist plans during the 1980s and 90s but once the station was restored in 1998, due to a generous donation from Historic Scotland, it became the new terminus for the Strathspey Railway.

The first part of the journey runs from Aviemore to Boat of Garten. Once past the outskirts of Aviemore and Dalfaber, passengers can enjoy the same kind of heather moors and woodland that are little changed since the 1860s. The Cairngorms are off to the east, partly bordered by the tall pine trees from a section of the ancient Caledonian Forest. Off to the west are the Monadhliath Mountains.

Nearer to the railway line travellers can spot

rowan, larch and Scots pine trees, while some of the wildlife includes red squirrels, roe deer and buzzards. Half way along the route lies Kinchurdy farm which has contained a settlement since medieval times.

The stations along the Strathspey Railway route are small and attractive, some being built at the opening of the railway in 1863 or at the end of the 1890s, while a few were rebuilt in more recent times.

Boat of Garten was the junction of the Speyside Branch of the Great North of Scotland Railway from 1866. During the Edwardian era, many villas were built in the village to accommodate staff and settlers.

Sometimes known as the 'Osprey Village', there is an observation hide for ospreys at Boat of Garten, about three miles from the village, which is maintained for the Protection of Birds. The large birds-of-prey have been returning to the loch side since the 1950s.

As the train chugs its way along from the station, passengers can look out for the ice house at Milltown of Drumullie. Built into a bank, the ice house stored ice from the nearby mill pond during the winter to keep salmon and food cool throughout the summer months.

The railway line eventually passes through the more agricultural landscape of Strathspey, and the River Spey itself is visible to passengers as the train steams alongside it. The hillside rises above Nethy Bridge and the pretty 18th century town of Grantown-on-Spey.

The present Broomhill Station was rebuilt in 1997 on the original foundations. It used to be the station which took the timber traffic that once floated down the Spey, but it then became famous as the railway station, Glenbogle, in the TV programme *Monarch of the Glen*. There is a pleasant walk along a footpath from Broomhill, by the side of the River Spey, to Nethy Bridge Village, where there are shops and a visitor centre.

Although the train terminates at Broomhill, they are hoping to extend it to a new terminus at Grantown-on-Spey in the near future, which will let passengers enjoy another three and a half miles of the leisurely steam train journey.

The Strathspey Steam Railway is a wonderful day out for all the family. There are special events run throughout the year. One special treat is the Traditional Sunday Lunch on certain Sundays and Fridays which is served at the passengers' tables. It is an ideal way to experience the nostalgia of steam train journeys as they were in the past.

The Jacobite Steam Train
West Highland Railway

'The Jacobite' steam railway journey from Fort William to Mallaig was popular long before it became a famous route for the Hogwarts Express in the Harry Potter films.

One of the most picturesque railway journeys in Scotland, the legendary steam train begins its journey on 'The Road to the Isles' at the sound of a whistle from Fort William station in the West Highlands. The station itself is in the shadow of the mighty Ben Nevis, the highest mountain in the United Kingdom.

It is known as the Jacobite Steam Train, not surprisingly, because it passes through much of the area associated with Bonnie Prince Charlie (Prince Charles Edward Stuart) during the Jacobite Rebellion.

The following points of interest are some of the historic highlights mentioned in the excellent little route guide given to passengers. The Gaelic names and their meanings only add even more enjoyment to the romance of the journey.

The whole rail journey from Fort William to Mallaig is a 42-mile tour through some of the most dramatic scenery in this part of Scotland. One of the first interesting sights comes as the train crosses the 1901 swing bridge over the Caledonian Canal. Linking the east and west coasts of Scotland, and designed by Thomas Telford, the canal was opened in 1822 with a series of eight locks, known as Neptune's Staircase.

The next section takes passengers past the Field of the Dead at Corpach, where the bodies of Highland nobility were kept on the way for burial to the island of Iona. Along the six-mile stretch of Loch Eil, seventeen sea walls protect the railway from gales, while a little further on the mountains rise up to 2,900 feet.

Bonnie Prince Charlie stayed the night in this area in 1745. Evidently, he picked a wild white rose to put in his hat, and thus it became known as the White Cockade, which symbolised the Jacobite cause and identified those who followed it.

Along the sixteen miles of *Finnan's Glen* is the stunning 416-yard Glenfinnan Viaduct built by Robert McAlpine, which began construction in the late 1890s. Reaching 100 feet high, with twenty-one arches, it is built on a 12-chain curve.

Made even more famous by the Harry Potter films which show the Hogwarts Express chugging across the Viaduct, it is a magnificent sight. With views to Loch Shiel on one side and the hills on the other, it is a photographer's dream to capture the train on the curve with steam trailing from the engine.

The train stops at Glenfinnan on the outward journey for about twenty minutes. The restored station is a museum and the Glenfinnan Monument, which commemorates the raising of Bonnie Prince Charlie's standard, is within walking distance of the station. This is also a good viewpoint for motorists to stop and watch for the arrival of the steam train across the viaduct.

The next stretch of the railway reaches a summit at the twin tunnels of the Crag of Goats, before making its descent along a mountain ledge to Loch Eilt. On the way, it passes a cave where Bonnie Prince Charlie is supposed to have hidden after his defeat in 1746.

The journey to Lochailort travels past the first Commando training centre, dating from 1940, and the biggest camp for the navvies who worked on the construction of the railway. It also boasted the first fully manned hospital set up on a British construction site. Some miles on, as the train reaches Polnish, there is the lovely hillside church of 'Our Lady of the Braes', which starred in the film *Local Hero*.

Loch nan Uamh (loch of the caves) is where Bonnie Prince Charlie landed in 1745 from a French frigate. Unfortunately, he departed again in 1746, after his defeat at Culloden. This is the steepest part of the line, at Beasdale Bank, where the gradient is 1 in 48 to reach the summit. This is followed by the longest tunnel on the line which stretches to 349 yards on the way to Arisaig.

Known as Britain's most westerly station, Arisaig is unique in having a mild climate due to the Gulf Stream, which allows it to grow sub-tropical plants, and its Gaelic name means 'the safe place', which seems very fitting! The islands of Rhum and Eigg are visible from here. Some miles further on are the famous Morar white sands where *Local Hero* and *Highlander* were filmed.

As the train chugs its way towards its final destination, it passes along by the Sound of Sleat, with the Isle of Skye and its Cuillins mountain range in the distance and there is another couple of miles of scenery before the train reaches Mallaig, which means Bay of the Gulls.

Passengers have about an hour and forty minutes to enjoy the pretty little fishing village of Mallaig, which dates from the 1840s, before the return journey. Although a busy terminal for the car ferries to Sky and the Outer Hebrides, there are restaurants, a Marine World and a Heritage Centre of interest around the village.

A day out on the Jacobite Steam Train is an

unforgettable experience, through dramatic mountains, past deep lochs and across the stunning Viaduct.

It may be an area of great historical interest with its connections to Bonnie Prince Charlie, but there is no doubt that the Harry Potter films have added to the attraction of one of the Greatest Train Journeys in the World.

The Lafaruk Madonna

Seldom do the ravages of war result in something so beautiful and touching that thousands of people continue to marvel at it today. The Lafaruk Madonna is a story of hope as well as a thing of beauty and a joy forever.

Now hanging in the refurbished Kelvingrove Art Gallery and Museum in Glasgow, the set of three paintings had the most inauspicious of beginnings.

One year into World War II, Italy entered the fray to become Britain's enemy. By August 1940, Britain was facing a loss of naval supremacy. Control of the southern approaches to the Suez Canal was threatened by an Italian conquest of British and French Somaliland.

At the same time, Italian forces were invading northern Greece but were ultimately unable to sustain their offensive. In the end, the Italians were defeated both in the Balkans and in Northern Africa and, by February 1941, several thousand Italian prisoners were rounded up by British forces.

It was in one of the subsequent British prisoner-of-war camps that the story of the Lafaruk Madonna had its birth.

Those Italian prisoners who had the good fortune, as it turned out, to be held at the Lafaruk camp near Berbera (in present day Somalia) were happy enough to be under the command of a Captain Alfred Hawksworth, an officer who determined that his prisoners would be treated well.

Captain Hawksworth understood that the Italian men's religious faith was of the utmost importance to them, especially the image of the Madonna. He therefore permitted his prisoners to express their devotions in a small mud hut converted into a chapel in the prison grounds.

One of the prisoners was gifted as an artist, and he was allowed to put his talent to good use to create a focal point for their worship. There was, however, one small problem. There was no canvas for his work.

Undaunted by such a minor setback, Giuseppe Baldan made do with what was available. Using the back of old, discarded flour bags, he began to paint. His resulting triptych of beauty and colour must surely have given the men great hope and comfort during a time of war and loss of freedom.

The smaller central painting shows the Virgin Mary gazing adoringly at her son, the baby Jesus, with an olive sprig in her hand. The paintings on either side depict an angel looking towards these central figures. In the background of all three paintings are the huts and arid ground of the war camp with a suggestion of mountains on the horizon.

The triptych is in rich shades of blue, red and green with touches of white, incorporating the colours of the Italian flag. They were hung in pride of place at the front of the chapel where the Madonna and child might inspire the Italian prisoners to pray for and remember their families at home.

Harry Dunlop, of Glasgow Museums, who was largely responsible for the display in Kelvingrove, suggests that the Madonna, the ultimate mother figure, had a more fundamental meaning for these men far from home.

In typical Glasgow parlance he reckoned that the Madonna "reminded the poor men of their mammies!" Since the prisoners were far from their own country, with no certainty they would ever return home, he probably has a point. It must have been comforting to gaze upon such a revered mother and baby while praying she would get them home eventually.

The inclusion of the Madonna's olive branch, the symbol of peace and reconciliation, no doubt reinforced their hope that they really would be reconciled with their families one day.

Yet the paintings and the story could have been forever lost.

When the camp was finally disbanded, the Somali

soldiers who had helped to keep order destroyed the chapel and deliberately slashed the paintings.

It is difficult to understand why they should perform such a spiteful and unnecessary act of desecration and destruction when it hardly mattered at that stage. Perhaps they had been jealous of the prisoners' faith and fortitude. Fortunately, however, the Italian soldiers managed to rescue what was left of the paintings and gave them into the safe keeping of their esteemed Captain Hawksworth.

And so again, the story might have ended. Then, in 1965, Captain Hawksworth tried to return the paintings to the Italians. Instead of their eager acceptance of them, Captain Hawksworth received the following letter from the camp interpreter, Luigi de Giovanni:

'I have appreciated your idea of bringing back to Italy the sacred paintings of captivity we had entrusted to you… but you must keep them for ever as a gauge of gratitude and love by the 35,000 people who owe you, beyond their life, the dignity of human treatment.'

Although there are a few torn-off pieces missing from the angel paintings, and perhaps because of it, the Lafaruk Madonna is a testament to the resilience of the human spirit and the triumph of human kindness over the ravages of war. Their very existence and incredible survival must surely be a symbol of hope to all who look upon them.

It seems fitting that Luigi de Giovanni and Captain Hawksworth continued to write to each other and, after all thought of war had been put behind them, they finally met up on holidays with their families. When Captain Hawksworth died in the 1970s, his wife generously donated the paintings, and story, to Kelvingrove.

Nowadays, people from all parts of the world come to admire the wonderful exhibits at this famous art gallery and museum. The valuable and world-renowned impressionist paintings are among the favourites of many.

Yet, within an almost hidden alcove to one side of these masterpieces, we can gaze upon this special display; of a twentieth century work that has left us something more valuable.

The Lafaruk Madonna, which began with the enforced meeting of men from opposing sides of a devastating war, leaves a legacy of peace and reconciliation to our own uncertain world.

Published in The Oldie

Britannia Panopticon: Britain's Oldest Surviving Music Hall

Hidden amongst the old buildings of the Trongate in Glasgow is a remarkable old Victorian music hall known as the Britannia Panopticon.

You would never know it was there, situated above a very modern amusement arcade, although an observant passer-by might look up and notice the beautiful façade of an older building. Like much of Glasgow, the architecture is often most impressive above eye-level.

A few years ago, I was lucky enough to be given a tour of the interior along with members of my writing group by the woman who brought it to life again, Judith Bowers.

Once we located the building, it was a matter of going right through the amusement arcade to find the stairs up to the hidden world of the old music hall. It was like stepping back into the past where Judith gave us an enthusiastic run-down on the building's fascinating history and her passion for restoring as many of the original features as possible.

Standing within the darkened, Victorian surroundings, my imagination soon peopled the seats with the raucous audience that once watched the acts below, although at times the audience itself seems to have been a part of the drama! Judith had us enthralled with some of the less salubrious stories from those days.

We were allowed to stand on the restored stage that once held the great Stan Laurel and it was wonderful to hear that it is now welcoming modern acts once again. The memorabilia set out on tables, which includes items actually discovered under the old balcony seats, gave a flavour of the Victorian theatre and the type of entertainment brought to the Glasgow Trongate of long ago.

Beginning life as a warehouse, the original Britannia Music Hall went through several changes of use from its opening in 1857. The first renovation was to the outer façade when the architects Thomas Gildard and Robert H.M. MacFarlane redesigned the front of an old warehouse. Their elegant classical design with cherubs celebrated Glasgow's reputation as the second city of the Empire. The date, MDCCCLVII, was carved in Roman numerals into the stone beneath the apex.

When John Brand took over the building, he named it the Britannia Music Hall after the statue of Britannia that stood within sight of the doors at

Glasgow Cross. In its early days, the music hall attracted mostly male customers, not least for the titillation of watching dancing girls and female acrobats. The only women who entered were generally those soliciting a paying customer for the evening, in a dark corner of the theatre.

By the 1860s, however, Brand upgraded the Britannia to attract a family audience and added wooden pews to the balcony and a proscenium arch above the stage. There was now a strict door policy and bills were printed with the words: "No ladies admitted unless accompanied by gentlemen". Up to 1,500 people attended the daily shows which were now regarded as a family treat.

As the popularity of the Britannia Music Hall increased, it attracted many singers, dancers and an early type of stand-up comedian who poked fun at famous people and everyday situations, often in comedy songs. One of the first famous acts was Dan Leno with his clog dancing, before he moved on to pantomime.

At the end of the 1860s, the music hall came under the ownership of the Rossboroughs. The husband and wife team overhauled and upgraded the building before reopening it to critical acclaim. Over the following few years, burlesque became popular and some of the stars performing at the Britannia included Marie Lloyd, Marie Loftus and male impersonator, Vesta Tilley.

The next owner of the Britannia, William Kean, closed the building for several months in 1896 to modernise it and install the new electric light.

When it reopened later that year, it showcased a new form of entertainment called, the 'Cinematographe of Animated Pictures: the Marvel of the Nineteenth Century'.

The moving pictures were a great success and the projectionist and supplier of the films, Arthur Hubner, eventually took over the Britannia in 1897.

One of the most enduring stars of the Britannia was the famous performer Harry Lauder, who went on to become a legend in London as well as Glasgow, with songs such as: 'A Wee Doch and Doris' and 'Roamin in the Gloamin'.

By 1905, the Britannia had acquired a new staircase and yet another new manager. Albert Ernest Pickard already owned an old Waxworks and American Museum when he took over the neighbouring music hall. He closed the building and reopened it in May 1906 as the Britannia and Grand Panopticon, to instant success. In addition to the variety entertainment, Pickard offered wax tableaux, including a torture chamber, an electric rifle-shooting machine and paintings and statues.

The Panopticon part of the name caused some confusion, especially when it had previously referred to a circular type of prison in the 1800s. But its Greek roots were 'everything' from the *pan*, and 'visible' or 'seen' from the *optikan*. Pickard advertised the Panopticon as a place where people could 'see everything' for the ticket price.

On acquiring the basement of the building in 1908, he opened his 'Noah's Ark', which included forty-two animal cages holding bears, monkeys, birds and reptiles. When the bear managed to escape and growled at passers-by in the Trongate, Pickard turned it into a publicity stunt and shot the animal. Another popular draw was the assortment of human novelties in the attic space and adjoining museum, which included bearded ladies and tiny men.

One half of the famous comedy duo, Laurel and Hardy, the young sixteen-year-old Stan Laurel (born Jefferson) made his debut on the stage of the Panopticon in 1906 and went on to be a box-office hit. Stan eventually became successful in America, obtaining a film contract with Universal Studios. It was during this period he met Oliver Norvall Hardy, and the rest is history.

One of the first matinee idols, Jack Buchanan also made his comedy and singing debut at the Panopticon, which was less successful than his eventual film career. Although he enjoyed live stage work, his fame increased when he went to Hollywood in 1929 and appeared in the new talkies with actors such as Fred Astaire and Cyd Charisse.

The Panopticon continued to delight audiences well into the 1920s, but cinema soon took the place of the old music hall and the basement zoo was finally closed. Pickard added a new Art Deco auditorium and the latest technology, reopening it as the Tron

Cinema. It soon reverted to the Panopticon and there were no further renovations to the Victorian wooden benches and facilities.

In the spring of 1938, the Panopticon closed its doors and the building was sold to a tailor. The great days of the Britannia Panopticon Music Hall were apparently over. Until Judith Bowers discovered it by accident one day. Through her tenacious curiosity and passion for this lost Victorian treasure she gradually stirred interest in the abandoned music hall on the upper floor.

Eventually, the Britannia Panopticon received wider publicity after appearing on the BBC Restoration programme in 2003. They may not have won, but the doors were opened to the public for the first time in sixty years or so and the songs from the old music hall played to an appreciative modern audience.

As we left this fascinating old theatre, I imagined the sound of applause and calls from the balcony following us back to the modern world.

Thankfully, the ghosts of the past have now been superseded by a new era for the Britannia Panopticon, bringing music hall back to the Glasgow Trongate.

You can read the full story of the Panopticon's revival in Judith Bower's book, *Glasgow's Lost Theatre: The Story of the Britannia Music Hall*, published by Birlinn.

Author's Note

I hope you enjoyed these articles about various aspects of Scotland's heritage, and thank you for reading them. With non-fiction writing, I usually provide my own photographs to illustrate the articles and you can view a further selection of them on my website.

You can also subscribe to my newsletter from there if you would like to be kept up to date with news and occasional competition giveaways.

www.rosemarygemmell.co.uk

Published Books

Highcrag
The Highland Lass
Return to Kilcraig
Dangerous Deceit
Midwinter Masquerade
Mischief at Mulberry Manor
Pride & Progress
Venetian Interlude
Christmas Charade
The Aphrodite and Adonis Touch

Short Story Collections
Beneath the Treetops
End of the Road
Two of a Kind

Non-Fiction Articles
Scotland People and Places

Middle Grade Children's Fiction
Summer of the Eagles
The Jigsaw Puzzle
The Pharaoh's Gold

About the Author

Rosemary Gemmell lives in central Scotland. She is a prize-winning freelance writer of short stories, articles and poetry in UK magazines, online and abroad. She also writes contemporary and historical novels.

Rosemary is a member of the Society of Authors, the Romantic Novelists' Association and the Scottish Association of Writers.